Tying Trout Flies

Lures, Nymphs and Buzzers

Freddie Rice

*Member of the Association of Professional
Game Angling Instructors – Fly Dressing*

*National Angling Council Instructor, Grade I,
including Fly Dressing Trout and Salmon*

B.T. Batsford Ltd · London

Acknowledgements

To all the following I would like to express my sincere thanks: Alan Bramley of Partridge of Redditch for his unstinting support over a long period, freely given even at times of great pressure from his hook making business; Trevor Coxon, for long an angling companion and personal friend, for his technical expertise and attention to detail in producing the colour photographs; Peter, of Veniard Ltd, for generous support; the staff of the Dittons Public Library for whom no request of mine ever received less than undivided attention, and for their helpful advice on questions of research; all those from whose work quotations have been selected and quoted herein; the very many fly-tying students it has been my pleasure to meet over the years, whose searching questions on the subject have, time and again, reinforced in my mind the problems faced by beginners; finally, to my wife, Doris, whose unrelenting chivvying kept my nose to the grindstone and whose efficient organizing ability and attention to detail brought order out of chaos and this book to fruition, as well as to my son, Graham, whose ever-present support and journalistic experience and advice were invaluable. Thank you all.

Long Ditton

Freddie Rice
September, 1991

First published 1993

© Freddie Rice, 1993

All line illustrations by Freddie Rice, photographs by Trevor Coxon.

Typeset by Servis Filmsetting Ltd, Manchester

and printed in Hong Kong

Published by
B.T. Batsford Ltd
4 Fitzhardinge Street
London W1H 0AH

A catalogue record for this book is available from the British Library

ISBN 0 7134 6582 4

Contents

Introduction

Angling

Cards, Dice, and Tables pick thy purse;
　　Drinking and Drabbing bring a curse,
Hawking and Hunting spend thy chink;
　　Bowling and Shooting end in drink,
The fighting-Cock, and the Horse-race,
　　Will sink a good Estate apace,
Angling doth bodyes exercise;
　　And maketh soules holy and wise;
By blessed thoughts and meditation;
　　This, this is Anglers' recreation!
Health, profit, pleasure, mixt together,
　　All sport's to this not worth a feather.

Thomas Barker, *The Art of Angling*
(1651). It comes from the dedication to
Edward, Lord Montagu who was
afterwards Earl of Sandwich and Pepys's
patron.

The knowledge and competence of the average fly fisher of the present day is greater than it has ever been before. Some of that increased competence has undoubtedly been brought about by improvements in rods, reels, lines and leaders. Floating, sink tip, intermediate, sinking and specialized lines have enabled anglers to improve their casting so as to get the fly to the required area and depth. Tapered leaders ensure a better turnover and assist in avoiding the age-old fault of the fly and leader landing in a heap. I do not think it can be denied that the competent caster, using modern tackle, will put the fly down not only where he wants it without recourse to false casting, but also in the fashion least likely to alarm the fish.

In addition, the wide variety of literature on the subject, the availability of video films and the number of courses of instruction both in angling techniques and fly-tying, have undoubtedly contributed to the wider dissemination of knowledge on the subject.

It is an indisputable fact that the only fly capable of catching the fish is the one in, or on, the water and it is towards the fly that this book is directed and to those anglers really interested in obtaining the maximum enjoyment from their fishing.

The problem is – which fly? It seems clear that the only way to make a decision is to go to a water and experiment; but these days, when most seem able to spare little time for such things, the alternative is to rely to a large extent on the views of the 'experts' who spend much of their time testing theories.

Thus the angling magazines set out month by month the latest offerings, usually with some reference to the water at which the flies were tested. Now, if an article indicates that the fish were lining up in droves to have a go at this month's offering and enticing shots of big fish are displayed, is it not natural that many anglers will dash off to tackle shops to buy the ready-tied fly or to get the materials to tie it up themselves? In subsequent weeks thousands of anglers may be using the fly. Because so many are doing so, many more fish are caught, word spreads that the fly is catching fish all over the place, vast numbers of additional anglers use the fly, the fly becomes the wonder of the moment until – eureka! Another 'killer' fly surfaces in print and off it all goes again!

In this book I have tried to provide a fairly wide range of patterns, some new, some old but all, in my opinion, worthy of merit. We all have favourite patterns in which we place great faith and which we fish with confidence. The method of tying them, and the materials needed, are readily called to mind for these favourites but, for others, it is necessary to turn up a work of reference. For those using this book I have not only provided a list of the materials needed in order of use but for each fly have also provided a numbered text, supported by similarly numbered line drawings clarifying each operation to be performed. To supplement this a colour photograph, of a size to allow for complete clarity, is provided for each pattern listed. This, I think, provides the next best thing to personal tuition.

In the establishments which cater for the angler who has not yet joined the ranks of the fly-tyers will be found countless patterns, some designed by people well known in the current angling press, others by anglers of yesteryear. All are the result of work at the fly-tying bench attempting to copy nature or to accentuate certain aspects of size, colour, form, or simply to provide for ease of production.

Is the non-flytyer not missing out on the pleasures of bringing to fruition his own offerings, be they reproductions of the designs of others or original patterns? I think they are. In the late autumn particularly, when the rod arm is subject to involuntary movement brought about by the memory of a particularly pleasurable catch, then is the time to get the grey matter buzzing whilst sitting at the fly-tying bench.

No-one can force anyone to believe that fly-tying is an absorbing interest, but those who practise it are hooked on its pleasures and anticipations and I wish every angler would at least attempt it. As one who has been tying for a great many years I can say that there is no greater pleasure than in designing a hooky fish food, varying it if need be by trial and error at the bench or the waterside using the fish as guinea-pigs, and then settling for *one's own* pattern: this can thereafter be fished with confidence enhancing personal pride when the catch lies there on the bank. Confidence is all!

The fly-tyer should attempt to produce a range of artificial flies which resemble the general shape and colouration of the natural insect or fish, accentuating perhaps certain features, If need be, to improve the deceit. Size must also be considered and one pattern produced in several sizes pays dividends as do colour variations.

One sees every month, in the magazines which cater for our sport, more and more of what I would choose to describe as 'designer flies', that is, patterns which have not been based on natural insects or fry but on what the inventor's brain tells him should be attractive to fish. This is nothing new for we have all read about the chap who, having a few odds and ends lying on the bench at the end of a fly-tying session, sets to with those bits and pieces and produces a fly which he then adds a title – Punters' Pick or some such name. This fly, then taken to the water, is found by its inventor to be enthusiastically welcomed by the fish. Now it may be, and probably has been, that, over the years, quite a number of flies 'invented' in that way have turned out to be superb fishcatchers. I would have more confidence, I think, if the name of the inventor told me that he was an angler or fly-tyer with a long standing reputation.

I have chosen to assume that the reader possesses a certain amount of fly-tying knowledge but even a beginner should be able to produce a very acceptable fly by following the numbered operations supplied for each pattern.

In the following pages will be found patterns of lures, nymphs, buzzers and emergers. Every one may be tied and used with confidence since they have been evolved by well known and experienced anglers. However, they represent but a tiny few of the untold numbers used worldwide, every one of which, it might encourage you to remember, was born at the fly-tying bench.

WAYS AND MEANS

GENERAL FLY-TYING PROCEDURE

It is necessary that flies be tied to a general procedure. In tying a nymph, the following is one of the common methods of proceeding:

1   Secure the thread to the hook and wind it to above the barb
2   Incorporate any necessary body weight
3   Tie in the tail
4   Tie in the ribbing
5a Tie in the body material unless this is dubbing
5b If dubbing is used, apply the dubbing to the thread ready for winding on
6   Wind the body, whether using dubbing or other material
7   Wind on the ribbing
8   Tie in any materials for (a) thorax and (b) wing cases
9   Wind on, or dub on and wind, the thorax
10 Pull over and tie down the wing case material behind the eye
11a Tie in and wind any hackle specified, or
11b Tie in any bunch of fibres specified as a 'beard' hackle
12 Tie in and wind on any special head
13 Wind a neat thread head
14 Add whip finish and trim out thread
15 Varnish the head and whipping

I stress that this is but one of the many general procedures. As the materials are incorporated, or wound on, it is essential that the thread first be moved to the new position to allow that material to be secured to the shank when the winding on movement ends. You will observe that for this nymph we begin to incorporate materials at the tail; that

is, above the barb and progressing towards the eye and this applies to many, but by no means all, flies. In this way, each additional material incorporated covers the turns of thread used to tie it in and, since the final operation is to wind the head and whip finish, none of the tying-in joints will show unless the work is sloppily or carelessly handled.

Be painstaking in your work and good results will follow.

Securing the Thread to the Hook Shank

The initial step in tying any fly is to secure the thread to the hook shank in a position appropriate to the first operation called for in the dressing. There are at least two ways of doing this. One way is to hold the bobbin holder in the right hand and, with about 50mm (2in) of thread extending beyond the end of the spigot, hold this end between the left index finger and thumb. Place the thread (which is between the hands) behind the hook shank. Keep the left hand steady and, with the right hand, wind two or three close turns progressing slightly to the right. This done, reverse direction and wind three turns progressing slightly to the left and over the existing three turns. This should hold firmly and can be tested simply by allowing the bobbin weight to hang by the tyings.

Tying Off

This is the term commonly used to denote that, once material is tied in and dealt with in accordance with the tying operation, two or three turns are taken round the material finally to secure it to the shank before trimming out waste ends and moving on to the next operation. Don't overdo these securing turns as each turn you make is simply adding bulk and on a very small fly this is an important consideration.

Dubbing

Dubbing is the term used to describe the procedure used by fly-tyers to apply furs, etc., to the thread to be wound round the shank to provide whole fly bodies, tags, thorax or heads. This dubbing procedure is carried out as follows. First wax a short length of thread if pre-waxed thread is not in use. Pick, cut, chop, tease out or pull apart the material you intend to use then, with about 50mm (2in) of thread between the bobbin holder spigot and the position where the thread is secured to the hook shank, pick up a little dubbing, place it on the ball of the right forefinger and then place finger and fur behind the thread. Press the right thumb down on to thread and dubbing, then move the thumb to the *left* and the forefinger to the *right*. Release the finger and thumb and repeat the rolling action adding more dubbing down the length of thread until the 50mm (2in) is closely surrounded with dubbing. The finger/thumb *must* be released after each movement or the dubbing just rolled on will be made very slack and may even be rolled off (see Fig. 1).

Dubbing Loop

Using this loop is a different method of preparing and applying dubbing. With the bob-

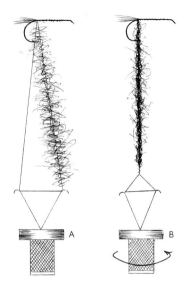

Fig. 2 Using a dubbing twister tool

Fig. 1 The hand dubbing process

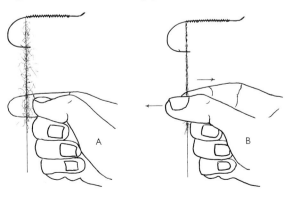

bin holder in the right hand and with the thread secured to the hook, pull about 200mm (8in) from the spool and place the left forefinger in the centre of that length of thread. Then, maintaining slight tension on the left forefinger in the loop, return the thread to the shank using the right hand and wind on two tight turns over the spot where the thread originally left the shank. Let the bobbin holder hang on the thread and insert a dubbing twister into the bottom of the loop formed. Dubbing is then stretched out in a narrow band on the bench before being placed between the two strands of thread forming the loop as in Fig. 2 above. When the dubbing is evenly distributed over the length of the loop, trim or re-adjust any which is of excessive width. Next, spin the dubbing twister in the fingers producing the required 'rope' but control the build up of twists using the fingers (see Fig. 2).

Excessive spinning is not conducive to good dubbing practice and could result in breakage of the thread loop. Loops which add weight can be produced by using fine copper wire or fuse wire to form the loop. Once spun, these 'rods' of dubbing can be stored for use when required.

Marabou Turkey Herls as Dubbing

A very useful dubbing can be produced by cutting some herls from the plume and then, with the tips of a small bunch held in the thumb and forefinger of the left hand and the butt ends in the right hand, break up the herls into short pieces 12mm ($\frac{1}{2}$ in) or, preferably, less which can then be treated in the same way as other dubbing material to wind the bodies of nymphs or other patterns.

HACKLES

Cock Hackles

Good quality cock hackles should be springy, quickly recoiling to the natural position if bent and released. They should have sparkle and a glossy sheen when examined against sunlight. The better the quality the narrower the hackle will be for its length, that is, the individual fibres branching from the central stem will be short yet reducing in size as they progress up the stem from base to tip. It used to be held that the best, glossiest, springiest hackles were obtained from mature birds about three years old but, provided the bird is in prime condition when killed, age now receives little consideration.

The most satisfactory way of buying hackles is to purchase a 'cape'. This is the description given to the skin cut from the area starting at the crown of the bird's head and stopping at the commencement of the saddle area. The shape of the skin so removed is cape shaped and provides hackles, ready sorted by nature, smallest at the crown area and increasing in size towards the saddle area. Thus, in one cape, hundreds of ready sized hackles are immediately available for choice. Whilst hackles can be purchased in packets, remember that first, someone else has chosen them and second, if they are specially selected of a size to match a particular hook size, you will pay appropriately.

There are other packeted hackles available which are of mixed size all jammed into one packet willy nilly. These are, of course, much easier on the pocket but, to find the one hackle needed at the moment, one has to sort through the whole packet which is not only time consuming but not a little irritating when it comes to putting them all back! Also a draught or a sneeze can, irritatingly, disperse them widely!

Hen Hackles

Capes are cut from the hen in the same way as the cock, but there the similarity ends. Where the cock hackle is long and spearlike, the fibres springy and glistening, the hen hackle is blunt ended and made up of soft, dull, heavily webbed fibres. Hen hackles are used mainly for wet flies since the heavy webbing absorbs water quickly.

Fig. 3 Matching hackle size to hook

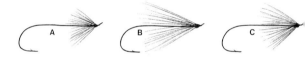

Matching Hackle to Hook

Suppose we were tying a lure for trout – say the Jersey Herd of Tom Ivens (page 33). When it comes to matching the hackle to the hook required for this fly, we have to consider just how far back from the eye of the hook the tips of the fibres are to reach to meet the usual tying. A hackle has to be selected which, when wound on, will allow the fibres to reach about half-way between the tying-in position and the joint of body and tail. To select a hackle at random could have one of the results shown below when A and B are misfits and not pleasing to the eye. Remember, also, that *the larger the hook number the smaller the hackle* generally required to match it (see Fig. 3 above).

Sizing Hackles

Where a pattern calls for a hackle behind the eye it is generally thought to require a hackle the fibres of which are one and one-third to one and one-half times the gape of the hook.

The simplest method of sizing a hackle is to bend the tip sideways round and down to the butt end. This will flare out the fibres and, if those projecting at the centre of the hackle are the right length for the fly being tied, then it can be used as fitting the hook. If the fibres are too long, a shorter overall length hackle is needed or, if too short, a longer overall length hackle should be selected. It is surprising how quickly this teaches the mind and eye to judge correctly.

Doubling Hackles

If one wishes to produce a fly with a hackle wound in open turns over almost the whole length of the body, the hackle for this purpose would, by tradition, be from a cock bird and would need to be tied in either by the butt end in a position behind the eye and wound from the eye to above the barb, or by the tip at the bend and wound from there to behind the eye. The reason for this is that it is desirable to have the fibres, which flare from the hackle as it is wound longest at the eye end to shortest above the barb, not only to look symmetrical but to ensure penetration of the hook. Furthermore, the fibres should all lean back towards the hook point to some extent: this can be achieved by 'doubling'.

The simplest way is to select a hackle where the fibres have been checked for size (as shown earlier). Suppose that it is to be wound as a wet fly head hackle, that is, wholly behind the eye of the hook. Tie it to

Fig. 4 Doubling a hackle

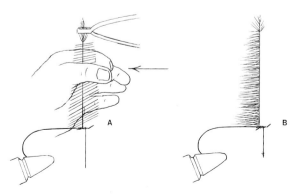

the hook shank by the butt end just behind the hook eye with the best side facing that eye. Clip a pair of hackle pliers on to the tip of the hackle and pull it up vertically. Then, holding the pliers in the right hand, use the forefinger and thumb of the left hand to stroke the fibres on both sides of the central quill towards the hook bend (i.e. to the left for right-handed tyers) applying particular pressure at the junction of fibres to the central quill as this is done (see Fig. 4).

When satisfied with the doubling, the hackle is ready for winding on. The doubling process, if carried out conscientiously, will ensure that, as the hackle is wound on, all fibres will lean in the right direction.

If, on the other hand, the hackle is required to be in open turns over the fly body, one way is to tie in the tip, not the butt end, at the position to be occupied by the first turn of ribbing tinsel from the bend. For the tip of the hackle to be hidden it must, of course, be tied in before the body material is wound on. With the hackle tip tied in, the body is wound on clockwise, at the completion of which the working thread should then be in position a little behind the eye. The doubling process is then applied as before *but more gently*, since the tip is rather weak. The hackle is then wound on followed by the tinsel wound anti-clockwise to support the turns of hackle.

It is important to remember that the central quill of the hackle must not be allowed to twist when winding it on for, if it does, it will nullify the object of the doubling process causing the fibres to spread untidily. Done correctly, however, the result should be a hackle wound in even, open turns, with all the fibres leaning in the desired direction.

Another way is to tie in the hackle behind the eye by the butt end, then double it and then wind it in open turns down the shank to the joint of the tail where the hackle tip is left hanging in the hackle pliers. The tinsel is then used to trap the tip of the hackle after which the tinsel is wound up the shank in open turns to behind the eye where it is tied off. The tip and butt end of the hackle tip can then be trimmed out.

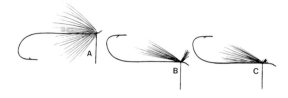

Fig. 5 Wound and beard (false) hackles

Fig. 6 Winding floss flatly

Wound, Beard (or 'False') Hackles

Hackles can be either wound on behind the eye (see A in Fig. 5) so that fibres surround the body and lean back toward the tail for a wet fly, or stand straight out from the shank for a dry fly; *or* a bunch of fibres can be tied in to project from beneath the body a little back from the eye and toward the hook point as in B, termed a beard (or 'false') hackle. For the latter method, fibres should be torn from a *large* hackle and, when these are tied in, the excess which protrudes well beyond the eye can easily be grasped and lifted to facilitate a clean cut close to the hook shank. Were short fibres used the excess would be too short to grip and time would be wasted fiddling with the removal of the short waste ends, as in C, in an effort to obtain a neat result.

Best Side – Poor Side

Every hackle has a 'best' side and a 'poor' side – the best side is the outer side as the feather lies on a live chicken. The difference between the two is quite marked for, whereas on cock hackles the best side is glossy and bright, the poor side is dull, lifeless and sometimes has a slightly powdery appearance. It is the best side which we value in fly-tying and hence the hackle is tied in to allow this side to be in view, that is, facing the hook eye.

Using Floss

Floss is made of silk or rayon. With both, rough skin on the fingers will be found troublesome. If handled carelessly individual strands can fray or break, resulting in a slightly ragged body. Gently rubbing the finger tips with pumice stone helps, as does moistening the floss.

Rayon rolls off the spool in straight fibres. Silk rolls off in a twist and, in order to produce a flat body of silk floss on a fly, the twist has to be removed from the length cut for use. The practice here is to tie in the silk at the necessary point on the shank and then untwist a section to enable it to be wound on *flatly*. You know when this is happening as both silk and rayon, when flat, leave the shank in an elongated 'V' shape as Fig. 6.

One also has to remember, with floss of silk and rayon, that each turn round the hook shank will put one twist in the floss and this must be corrected by giving the floss a twist in the opposite direction as each turn is made. If the floss ceases to leave the hook shank in the elongated 'V' described above, the floss is ceasing to be laid flatly on the shank and a bumpy body will result, spoiling the appearance of the fly.

Ribbing

When incorporating a ribbing, be it thread, tinsel or wire, into a dubbed body such as seal's fur, there is a tendency for the ribbing to sink deeply into the turns of dubbing if both the dubbing and the ribbing are wound on in the same direction, whether that be clockwise or anti-clockwise. Since a ribbing of tinsel serves the dual purpose of providing 'flash' and a protection against the turns of dubbing being broken up by the teeth of fish, all ribbing is best wound on counterwise to the dubbing. When using a springy dubbing material such as seal's fur, or if the dubbing is applied thickly (using many turns of thin dubbing) it will be found advantageous to use a wider tinsel than would normally be selected. This provides not only a greater band of protection to the dubbing but it also sinks less easily into the dubbing applied.

Winging

The general practice is to set the wing on the top of the shank for both wet flies and lures for trout. The problem for many tyers is keeping the wing fibres together and not spread round the shank. Such spreading results from allowing movement of the wing fibres in the direction of pull of the thread used to tie them in. The essential ingredient of success is to keep the wing fibres between the forefinger and thumb really *tightly* compressed otherwise some, or all, of the fibres will follow the pull of the thread as it is wound on and the fibres then move to some degree round the shank to the side of the hook furthest away.

The movement brought about by insufficient pressure being applied by forefinger and thumb can be particularly irritating when one wishes to position say, a separate bunch of black fibres over a bunch of yellow fibres, as in Goldie (page 28). What can happen is that the yellow fibres nearest the shank may sit well on top of the shank, but the black fibres being tied over them roll round to some degree due to slacking off of finger pressure and the black fibres then sit, not on top, but to the side, of the shank. Whether the fish nudge each other and chuckle at the result I doubt but one hasn't achieved one's objective and out-of-place fibres do not please the eye.

Keep the fingers very tightly compressing the winging fibres throughout the tying-in process. This requirement applies not only to winging fibres but *to any material one wishes to position on top of the hook shank.* I should stress that no amount of finger pressure will ever prevent the thread from moving through the clenched finger and thumb combination usually referred to as the 'pinch and loop' method, which should be used for all winging operations.

Wings and Tails of Turkey Marabou

To prepare marabou turkey plume for tying in, cut whatever quantity is considered needful for the fly in hand. In this connection may I say that for the tail of a nymph of the size of the Marabou Nymph (see page 16) a span of 12mm ($\frac{1}{2}$in) of the depth of the short fibres at the lower end of the plume would suffice whilst for the wing of a fairly large lure, such as Viva, (see page 15) at least 25mm (1in) of depth of the longer fibres in the centre of the plume are required. Prior to tying in a bunch of marabou herls, it is helpful if the *cut* ends are damped and rolled between the fingers for this joins the herls into a single block, making them much easier to handle. Try it!

Whip Finish

The most efficient and secure method of finishing a fly is to complete the final tying of the head with a whip finish. One method of achieving this can be accomplished quickly and neatly by hand with a little practice following the numbered steps in Fig. 7 below in which, for right-handed tyers, A is the thread in the left hand and B shows the turns of thread progressively applied to the hook by the right hand.

Alternatively, a whip finish tool can be purchased which will greatly assist those who find the process by hand somewhat difficult. Instructions are, of course, provided with the tool as to the method of use. I can only recommend to you, in the strongest terms, to acquire the practice of finishing every fly with a whip finish and not to rely on a series of half-hitches to complete the fly.

Fig. 7 The sequence of a whip finish

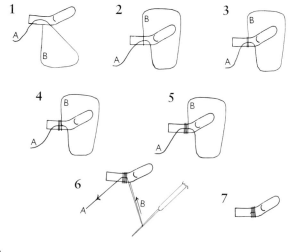

Dyeing of Materials

Nature does not provide a range of colours in the natural materials to suit all flies and it is therefore necessary to resort to the use of dyes. The aniline dyes available have greatly simplified the dyeing process which, in early times, was a very messy and hit-and-miss affair. Veniard's list 38 different colours of which five are fluorescent. When black dye is used it will be found that twice as much dye is required to obtain a dense 'colour' and the materials need to be left in the solution for a longer period. A couple of 15cm (6in) sauce-pans from a jumble sale; a half-ounce tub of the chosen dye; a strainer of decent size to facilitate removal of the material from the dye bath; a drop of vinegar (acetic acid) to set the colour; tap water and the kitchen stove and you are in business. Since full instructions as to use are provided with the dye, I will only stress the need to ensure that materials to be dyed, whether plumage or hair, need to be thoroughly degreased with detergent beforehand. A proprietary solution specially designed for the purpose is obtainable.

Two final words of warning: *Never* allow materials being dyed to boil in the dye as this can have a disastrous effect, leaving hackles or hair brittle, lacklustre and curled at the tips; *be sure* to clean the kitchen of dye splashes to avoid domestic upset!

'Gold', 'Silver' and Copper Heads

Since Roman Moser introduced his 'Gold Head Caddis' several years ago, a considerable number of patterns have appeared which feature the gold bead at the head of the fly. However, the special casting procedure which Moser formulated is known only through his video film entitled *New Ways of Fishing the Caddis*.

Hardly any fly which utilizes these heads makes any special reference to the purposely designed barbless hooks Moser introduced for use with his 'Gold Head Caddis' pattern. It is right that I should bring attention to this for the problem with the sizes of hook needed

is that the barbs will not pass through the hole in the 'gold' bead even though this hole is tapered from one side to the other. This means that, to use these beads on a barbed hook, one must first compress the barb. Unfortunately, this practice will, if carelessly carried out, seriously weaken the metal where the barb has been cut and, regrettably, that weakness is likely to show itself only when the point is under pressure from a hooked fish.

The special hooks which Moser designed are produced by Partridge of Redditch, the premier British hookmaker, under Code CS27 and are known as Roman Moser Barbless Dry Fly Hooks.

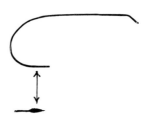

Fig. 8 Barbless point of a Partridge Code CS27 hook

In place of the normal barb, these hooks are provided with a specially designed point of the shape shown in Fig. 8. The special point passes easily through the hole in the bead whilst, more importantly from the fishing point of view, providing good holding power on a hooked fish.

In all patterns which incorporate these 'heads', the side of the bead which has the larger opening is that which is passed first over the hook point. It is then moved round the shank to a position hard up against the eye where it can be secured with bindings of thread on the bend side of the bead or glued in place with Araldite or Superglue. If the glueing method is adopted, it pays to deal with six or so in one session.

The advantage that these beads provide is that, once secured to the shank, they add weight at the *front* of the fly enabling one to easily control the way the fly trips along the bed of the stream.

Currently, not only are 'gold' beads marketed but 'silver' and copper beads also. The sizing of 'gold', 'silver' and copper beads is: Standard size (for hooks 6, 8 and 10) 4mm ($\frac{3}{16}$in) diameter; Ex. Small size (for hooks 10, 12 and 14) 2mm ($\frac{3}{32}$in) diameter.

Coloured Balls

These are of plastic, are produced in a number of colours including gold, silver and pearl but which, whilst providing the attractive glint at the eye of the hook, add very little weight. On these, however, provided that the barb will enter the hole on one side of the ball, being hollow, they present no problem passing over the barb or round the bend of the hook. They are not quite so easy to glue to the shank for being hollow, only the outside edges of the hole can be secured. They can, simply and successfully, be secured with turns of thread. I have yet to see coloured balls specified in size other than 'small' and 'medium'.

Polystyrene Balls

Remember, when using these balls for 'Booby' or 'Suspender' patterns, that fly-tying varnish, and spirit dyes in many pens used for colouring, will cause the balls to disintegrate. Better to use shaped plastazote if colouring is needed.

Twin Lead Eyes

These are shaped lead eyes joined together to enable them to be tied in, behind the eye of the hook, using a figure-of-eight binding. They are available in three sizes/weights:
Size 1 (Small) – diameter 3mm ($\frac{1}{8}$in) – weight 0.5g ($\frac{1}{64}$oz)
Size 2 (Medium) – diameter 4mm ($\frac{3}{16}$in) weight 1g ($\frac{1}{32}$oz)
Size 3 (Large) – diameter 5.5mm ($\frac{1}{4}$in) – weight 2g ($\frac{1}{16}$oz)

Lead Dumbells

These are the economy version of Twin Lead Eyes. They are used in the same way and are also bound to the hook using a figure-of-eight binding. For an example of their use in a fly see Hammerhead (page 30)

Experiment

Never hesitate to experiment with new materials or new ways of achieving one's objective. Not only is this enjoyable but frequently leads to very useful discoveries. Just consider that everything we currently know about fly-tying was, at some time in the past, unknown and had to be discovered. Nothing stands still and I am confident that much that we accept as standard fly-tying procedure now, will, in the not too distant future, be revised as new and, hopefully, better methods are discovered by someone experimenting. That someone could well be you!

The Patterns for Tying

In the next section, which provides sixty patterns for tying, I begin with three 'Easitied' flies. If you are not entirely confident in your fly-tying expertise, you may care to try these before moving on to the others.

Never tie just one of a pattern but do at least four and preferably six. There is good sense in this for, in repeating the same pattern a number of times, one can, using an honest, critical eye, see the faults which can be rectified in the next one tied. Thus one's confidence increases as improvement in the finished product is observed.

I have been tying for many, many years and have enjoyed every minute of it! For that reason I sincerely wish you a lifetime of enjoyable fly-tying, resulting, I hope, in numbers of good fish coming to your net!

PATTERNS

Easitied

MATERIALS

Hook	Partridge code D4A, size 8, 10 or 12
Thread	Brown, pre-waxed
Wing	Black or white marabou plume
Head	Fluorescent lime-green marabou plume

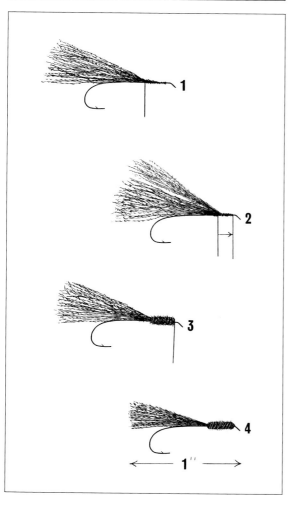

Tying Operations

1 Wind on a bed of thread over one-third of the level shank then tie in a small bunch of black or white marabou fibres to lie over the shank. Trim any excess at eye end.

2 At the same tying-in point, add a smaller bunch of fluorescent lime-green marabou fibres. Then wind the thread forward to behind the eye.

3 Twist the lime-green fibres into a rope and wind this back and forth creating the elongated head. Tie off behind the eye, trim out marabou waste, wind a neat head ending with a whip finish. Trim out the thread and varnish the head.

4 The overall length of the fly, including the wing, should be just about 26mm (1in). If the wing is overlong, gather the fibres tightly together at the required length and then twist off the excess with the thumb and forefinger. Finally, stroke the marabou fibres down and along the shank.

In the absence of fluorescent lime-green marabou for the head, fluorescent lime-green tow wool is a reasonable substitute.

2 *Marabou Nymph* (Freddie Rice)

MATERIALS

Hook	Partridge code H1A, size 12, 14 or 16
Thread	Olive
Tail	
Abdomen	Medium olive, black, brown or buff
Thorax	marabou plume
Wing cases	

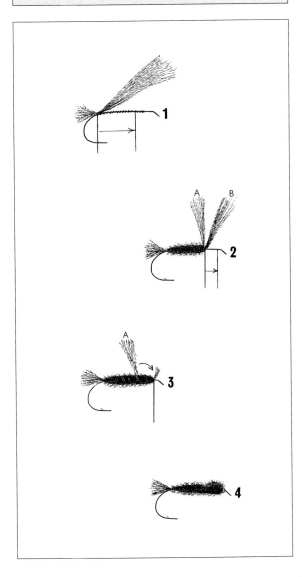

Tying Operations

1 Wind the thread from behind the eye to the start of the bend. Select a small bunch of marabou fibres, as long as possible, and tie these in above the barb to give an 8mm ($\frac{5}{16}$in) tail of the fine points. Then wind the thread two-thirds of the shank length towards the eye.

2 Twist the marabou fibres into a rope and wind it on until the thread is reached where it is secured to rise vertically. Next, split the marabou for the thorax and wing cases into two separate bunches A and B.

3 Twist bunch B into a rope and wind it on to behind the eye, forming the thorax. Secure it with the thread.

4 Pull bunch A down over the thorax to simulate wing cases. Tie off, trim out any excess marabou ends. Wind a neat head, whip finish and trim the thread. Finally, varnish the head.

This is a general pattern which, in various colours and sizes, provides a reasonable representation of a number of forms, is economical in materials and simple in its tying.

3 *Easitied Multi-buzzer* (Freddie Rice)

MATERIALS

Hook	Partridge code K2B Yorkshire Sedge, size 12 or 14
Thread	To match colour of abdomen
Abdomen	Swan, goose or heron wing herls, see table for colours
Thorax cover	As abdomen
Thorax	Rabbit, seal or mole fur, see table for colours
Head	Thread

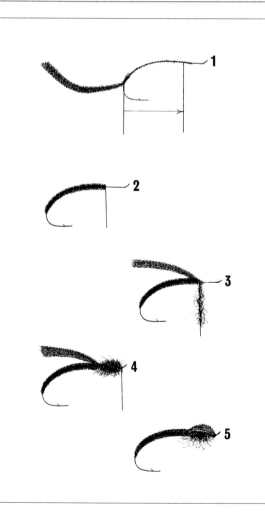

Tying Operations

1 Wind the appropriate colour thread from well behind the eye to half-way round the main hook bend, at which point tie in approximately four to six wing herls (for the abdomen) by their natural tips. Then wind the thread to the position shown.

2 Wind on the abdomen fibres in close turns to where the thread hangs. Remember that swan, goose and heron herls have a furry side and a smooth, shiny side, and it is, of course, the furry side which must be outward when winding them on. Tie off and trim out waste ends.

3 Tie in a fresh web of the same herls as used for the abdomen. Tie them in so that, in this case, the shiny side is uppermost.

4 Dub on the thorax fur, (many turns of thinly dubbed fur being better than a few turns of loosely dubbed thick fur) and wind this on forming the thorax. Leave room at the eye to tie down the thorax cover which is the next operation.

5 Pull the web of herls (the thorax cover) over the thorax and tie them down behind the eye. (You should observe that as the thorax cover herls have been pulled over, the furry side is now uppermost.) Trim any waste ends at the eye, wind a neat head ending with a whip finish, trim out the thread and varnish the whip. Finally, pick out, with a dubbing needle, a few of the longer hairs of the thorax to provide some resemblance to legs.

Variant	Thread	Abdomen	Thorax cover	Thorax
1	Orange	Orange	Orange	Orange
2	Olive	Olive	Olive	Olive
3	Black	Black	Black	Black
4	Claret	Claret	Claret	Claret

Lures

4 *Appetiser* (Bob Church)

MATERIALS

Hook	Partridge code D4A, long shank, down eye, size 6 or 8
Thread	Black
Tail	A spray of dark green and orange cock hackle fibres and silver mallard breast fibres, of equal amounts, mixed
Body	White chenille
Body rib	Fine oval silver tinsel
Beard hackle	Fibres from dark green and orange hackles and silver mallard breast feather, equal amounts, mixed
Wing	A generous spray of white marabou herl overlaid with a bunch of natural grey squirrel tail hairs
Head	Built up with thread, green bead eyes added (optional)

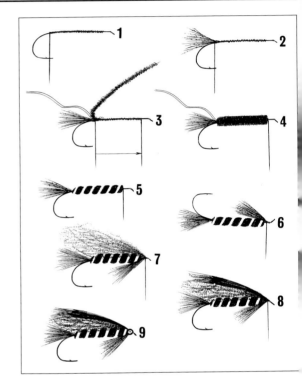

Tying Operations (colour plate on cover)

1 Wind on the thread from behind the eye to the start of the hook bend.

2 Tear out the green and orange hackle and silver mallard breast fibres, mix them and tie them in to extend about 7mm ($\frac{1}{4}$in) beyond the bend.

3 At the same point where the tail was added, tie in the tinsel and the chenille, in that order. Then wind the thread to 5mm ($\frac{3}{16}$in) from the eye.

4 Wind on the chenille in close, firm turns to where the thread hangs. Tie off and remove surplus chenille.

5 Wind on the tinsel in five or six open turns to the end of the chenille body. Tie off and trim surplus tinsel.

6 Turn the fly upside down in the vice. Tear out and mix the fibres described for the beard hackle and tie these in as shown in the drawing. Trim surplus ends obscuring the eye.

7 Turn the fly right way up in the vice. Select and tie in a generous spray of white marabou herl to reach the end of the tail. Trim waste over the eye.

8 Cut squirrel tail fibres of appropriate length. Hold the natural points in the left hand and flick out the loose shorter hairs. Then tie them in so that they reach just short of the tail end. Trim excess over the eye. Varnish hair roots.

9 Build up and whip finish the head with thread and then trim. As an option, tie in a green bead 'eye' on each side. Varnish the head to complete the fly. It works equally well without the eyes.

1 Viva Variant

2 Marabou Nymph

3 Easitied Multi-buzzer

5 Baby Doll (Brian Kench)

MATERIALS

Hook	Partridge code D4A or H1A, long shank, down eye, size 6, 8 or 10
Thread	Black
Body and tail	White nylon baby wool

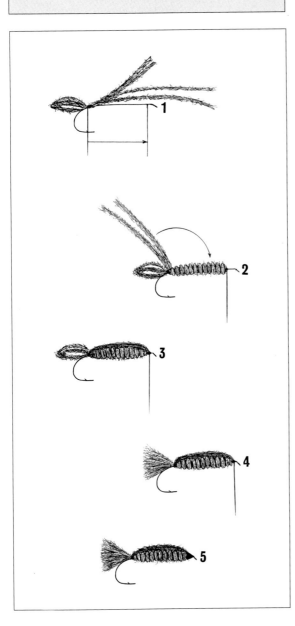

Tying Operations

1 Wind on a few turns of thread at the start of the bend. Cut two lengths of baby wool – one 5cm (2in), the other 10cm (4in) long. Fold both lengths in two centrally and tie them in securely where shown, leaving two loops overhanging the hook bend. Then press all four strands of wool away to the left to enable you to wind the thread in close turns up the shank until 3mm ($\frac{1}{8}$in) from the eye. Varnish those turns.

2 Segregate the two longest strands of wool and wind on both together in close turns to where the thread hangs. Tie off and remove surplus wool ends over the eye.

3 Now pull the remaining two shorter strands of wool, which were secured at the bend, directly over the body and tie down securely at the eye. Trim surplus wool over the eye.

4 Cut centrally the two loops which overhang the hook bend and fray these out for the tail.

5 Wind a neat head with the thread behind the hook eye, complete with a whip finish, trim out the thread and varnish both head and whip.

Variations

1 Peach wool replaces the white entirely.
2 Overbody wool changed to: Fluorescent lime-green, Fluorescent orange or Fluorescent red. See also Special Baby Doll on page 41.

6 *Black Chenille* (Bob Church)

MATERIALS

Hook	Partridge code D4A or H1A, long shank, down eye, size 6 or 8
Thread	Black
Tail	Black hackle fibres or a hackle tip
Body	Black chenille
Body rib	Silver tinsel, medium width
Beard hackle	Black hackle fibres
Wings	Four black hackles of even size in matched pairs

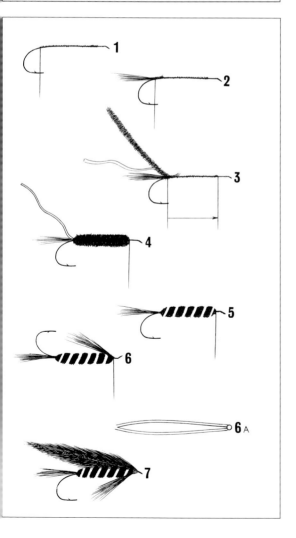

Tying Operations

1 Wind on the thread in close turns from 3mm ($\frac{1}{8}$in) behind the eye to the start of the bend.

2 Tie in the tail fibres on top of the hook shank. Trim the excess.

3 Tie in the silver tinsel where the tail fibres join the shank. Strip 6mm ($\frac{1}{4}$in) from the end of the chenille and tie this in at the same point, stripped end pointing to the eye. Then wind the thread to 3mm ($\frac{1}{8}$in) from the eye, tying down the stripped end of the chenille.

4 Wind on the chenille closely and evenly down the shank to where the thread hangs. Tie off and trim surplus chenille.

5 Wind on the silver tinsel tightly but in open turns to the eye end of the body. Tie off and trim surplus tinsel.

6 Turn the fly upside down in the vice. Tear a bunch of fibres from a fairly large black hackle and tie these in as a 'beard' as shown. Trim surplus ends to clear the hook eye. Then turn the fly over to original position.

7 Select four black hackles judging the size from the illustration. Place two on one side, two on the other, so that the pairs are back to back as in illustration 6A. With these in the left hand, position over the fly body and tie them in at the eye so that they lie as illustrated. Then trim the hackle ends, wind a neat head, add a whip finish, trim the thread and varnish the head, wing roots and whipping.

7 Dog Nobbler *(Trevor Housby)*

MATERIALS

Hook	Partridge code D4A, long shank, down eye or code A Standard, down eye, size 6, 8 or 10
Thread	To match body colour
Underbody or head	Heavy turns of lead wire at head or a split lead-substitute shot
Tail	Twice body length, ostrich or marabou, for colours see p. 94
Body	Chenille, for colours see p. 94
Hackle and rib	Palmered overbody as an option, (for colours see p. 94) with flat or oval tinsel for the rib

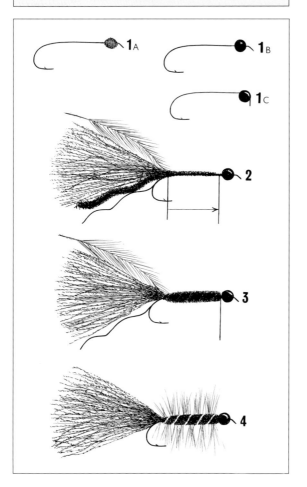

Tying Operations (for colours see p. 94)

1A If using lead wire, wind it on at the eye end only. You can judge your own weight for this.

1B If using a split shot, nip it on behind the eye.

1C This is the special 'Nobbler' hook with split shot on the bent portion, code K9A.

2 Wind the working silk from behind the lead to the start of the bend. Select the ribbing and the tail material. Tie the tail in so that it extends twice the length of the fly body, followed by the ribbing. Next strip the flue for 6mm (¼in) from the length of chenille and tie in the stripped end. If using a body hackle for the Tiger type, tie it in *by the tip* at the joint where the tail and chenille are tied in. Then wind the thread back to the bend side of the lead binding down any marabou ends.

3 Varnish the body (optional) and wind on the chenille in close, tight turns to behind the lead. Tie off and trim out the surplus end of chenille.

4 If a body hackle is tied in, use your fingers or hackle pliers to wind the hackle in even, open turns down to behind the lead. Tie off and then wind on the ribbing in five open turns. Tie off, trim tinsel and hackle ends, wind a neat head, whip finish and varnish the whip. Paint the weighted head (black, brown, orange or white) and add a dark eye on light paint or a light eye on dark paint.

Using the Fly

Trevor Housby uses a 9'6" rod, a size 9 line and only a 5 foot leader of 8lb. strain. He works the lure at high speed with a short, snatching style of retrieve, stripping about 15cm (6in) at a time. More action is added by a slight shake to the rod tip. It is this combined action that counts.

Variation

Black marabou and orange Crystal Hair tail, pearly fluorescent Body Wrap body with a badger or hot orange hackle wound as a collar behind the head. A special hook, Code K9A, is now commonly used. See illustration 1C.

5 Baby Doll

6 Black Chenille

7 Dog Nobbler

8 *Epsom Salt* (Freddie Rice)

MATERIALS

Hook	Partridge code D4A or H1A, long shank, down eye, size 6, 8 or 10
Thread	Black
Tail and overbody	Five to eight natural peacock herls
Body (rear two thirds)	Medium green or olive seal fur
Body (front one-third)	Red and orange seal fur mixed 50/50
Body rib	Flat silver tinsel, medium width
Head hackle	Hot orange cock hackle

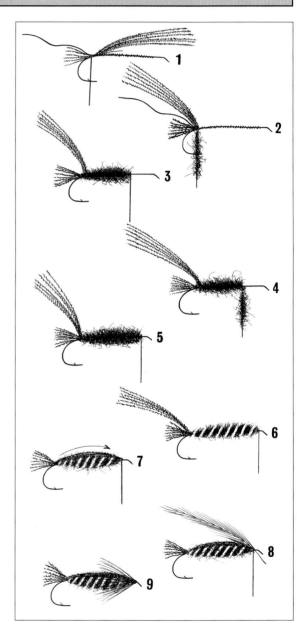

Tying Operations

1 Wind on turns of thread to the start of the hook bend then tie in the peacock herls (leaving a good 6mm ($\frac{1}{4}$in) protruding for tail) and the silver tinsel.

2 Coat the thread with wax and dub on the green seal fur.

3 Wind on the dubbed seal fur to form the rear two-thirds of the body.

4 Change the dubbing to the mixed red and orange seal fur, waxing a further length of thread if necessary.

5 Wind this on to form the front one-third of the body.

6 Pick up the tinsel and wind this on tightly in an open spiral to the head. Tie off with the thread and trim surplus tinsel.

7 Pull the peacock herls down over the whole body and tie them down at the head. Trim surplus herl ends.

8 Select a hot orange cock hackle of appropriate size and tie this in by the butt end at the head after stripping off the waste lower third.

9 Wind on the hackle (using hackle pliers or fingers) two or three turns only to form a collar as shown. Trim waste, wind a neat head, add a whip finish, trim out the thread and varnish the whip.

This is an excellent fly when fish are driving into the banks for fry since it represents the stickleback.

9 *Fireball* *(Freddie Rice)*

MATERIALS

Hook	Partridge code D4A, long shank, down eye, size 8, 10 or 12
Thread	Black
Tail	Black dyed squirrel tail
Body	Black floss
Rib	Flat silver tinsel, medium width
Wing	Hot orange marabou plume and six to eight hairs of hot orange Crystal Hair, well mixed
Hackle	Dark red saddle hackle, cock
Fireball Nosecone	Fluorescent scarlet floss
Head	Black

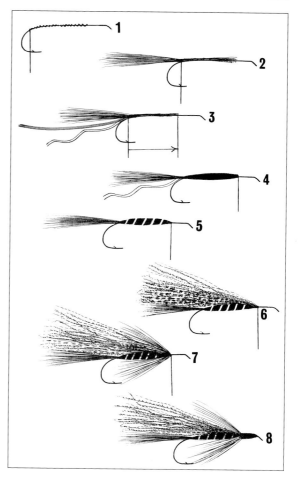

Tying Operations

1 Wind the thread from 6mm ($\frac{1}{4}$in) behind the eye to above the barb.

2 Cut the tail fibres long, tie these in securely above the barb with the cut end laid over the shank to a point where the thread was wound on initially.

3 Cut a 7.5cm (3in) length of tinsel, trim the end to a long point and tie this in at the tail joint. Follow this with 22.5cm (9in) length of floss at the same point then wind the thread to 6mm ($\frac{1}{4}$in) short of the eye, binding down the cut end of the tail.

4 Wind on the floss flatly, creating a smooth body, to where the thread hangs. Tie off and trim out excess floss.

5 Wind on the tinsel tightly in five open turns to the eye end of the body. Tie off and trim out excess tinsel.

6 Cut the marabou and Crystal Hair of sufficient length to reach from the tip of the tail to the eye end of the body where it is tied in to sit on top of the shank. Trim out any excess at the eye.

7 Tie in the hackle and wind it on so that the points reach just past the hook point. Trim any waste ends at the eye.

8 Cut a good length of floss, tie it in at the eye end of the body and wind it on to create the nosecone. Tie off, trim any excess, wind a neat head ending with a whip finish and trim out the thread. Add a small drop of varnish to the whip.

   This fly originated in 1987 preceding a trip to Grafham Water. It has proved exceptionally successful both in the large size as a single fly fished in lower and middle levels, and in size 12 as the point fly on a three-fly leader for surface work. One slight addition since then is a few Orange Crystal hair fibres mixed in with the marabou wing before tying in.

10 *Golden Bullet* (*Freddie Rice*)

MATERIALS

Hook	Partridge code D4AY, long shank, down eye, barbless size 10 or E3AY size 12 (size 10 most used)
Thread	Brown
Head	Polished solid brass, or silvered brass, bead
Tail	Orange marabou herl
Tag	Fluorescent red or lime-green wool or 'Glo-body'
Body	Fiery brown, amber or olive seal fur or Antron
Hackle	Red game, cock preferably, but hen will suffice

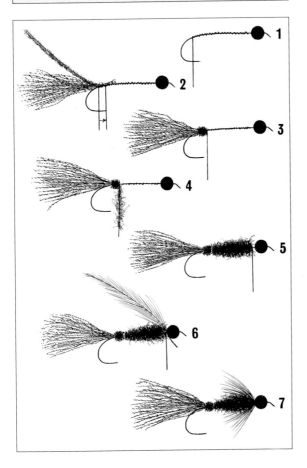

Tying Operations

1 Press the bead over the shank from point to eye and glue (Araldite or Superglue) in place. When the glue is set, wind the thread from a little behind the eye to the end of the level shank.

2 Cut a good tuft from a marabou plume and tie this in to reach a body length beyond the outside bend. Follow this with 5cm (2in) of selected tag material. That done, wind the thread forward 4mm ($\frac{3}{16}$in).

3 Wind on a short stubby tag then trim out any excess.

4 Dub the seal fur or Antron of the selected colour on to the thread ready for winding on.

5 Wind on the body dubbing to a little short of the brass bead. Tie off and remove any excess dubbing remaining on the thread.

6 Select the hackle, strip off the soft base fibres and tie in the butt end so that the flat of the hackle lies over the fly body.

7 Lift the hackle to the vertical and, using hackle pliers or fingers, wind it on three or four turns. Tie off and trim out hackle tip and butt end. Complete the fly by adding a whip finish behind the brass bead and trim out the thread.

When fitting the brass bead to the hook, if the D4AY or E3AY barbless long shank type hook is not used, then the barb should be a little depressed with a pair of pliers. Do this gently. Then press the brass bead over the point and up the shank to the eye. Apply a little Araldite or Superglue to the shank and roll the bead over it. Do six or more at a sitting – it pays.

8 Epsom Salt

9 Fireball

10 Golden Bullet

11 *Goldie* (Bob Church)

MATERIALS

Hook	Partridge code H1A, long shank, down eye, size 6, 8 or 10
Thread	Black
Tail	Yellow dyed cock hackle fibres
Body	Medium width gold lurex
Rib	Gold wire
Beard hackle	Yellow dyed cock hackle fibres
Wing	Squirrel tail, bleached and dyed yellow
Overwing	Squirrel tail, dyed jet black

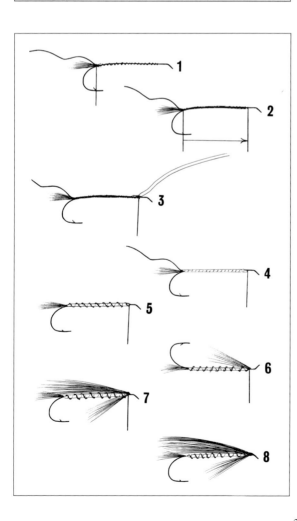

Tying Operations

1 Secure the thread behind the eye and run it in close turns to a point above the barb where 7.5cm (3in) of gold wire and a small bunch of yellow cock hackle fibres should be tied in to lie level with the shank.

2 Run the thread back up the shank ensuring that a smooth, even underbody for the Lurex is formed.

3 Cut 12.5cm (5in) of Lurex and trim one end to a long point. Catch in that point 3mm ($\frac{1}{8}$in) from the eye.

4 Wind the Lurex clockwise in close, edge to edge turns, to the start of the tail and then similarly back up the shank to where the thread hangs. Secure it there and trim out the excess.

5 Wind on the wire rib in open turns anti-clockwise up the body to where the thread hangs, secure it in place and trim out excess.

6 Turn the hook over in the vice. Cut a bunch of hackle fibres for the beard, ensure the tips are even and tie in the bunch so that the natural points reach two-thirds of the way to the hook point.

7 Turn the hook right way up. Cut the yellow wing fibres and tie these in on top of the hook so that the natural points reach the tips of the tail. Trim waste ends.

8 Cut the black overwing fibres, lay these squarely on top of the yellow wing and tie these in to provide the same length. Tie off, trim out excess hair ends over the eye, wind a neat head and whip finish. Trim out the thread and varnish the head three coats.

This is a popular reservoir lure, sleek and colourful, which has accounted for a great many fish. The Lurex body accents the yellow wing giving an all round aura which seems to be very attractive to trout.

12 *Grey and Red Matuka* (Dave Collyer)

MATERIALS

Hook	Partridge code A (Standard) or D4A long shank, down eye, size 6, 8 or 10
Thread	Black
Body	Silver-grey chenille
Body rib	Oval silver tinsel
Beard hackle	(Optional) Scarlet hackle fibres
Wing	Two or four round-ended white/brown hen pheasant flank feathers (but see options below)

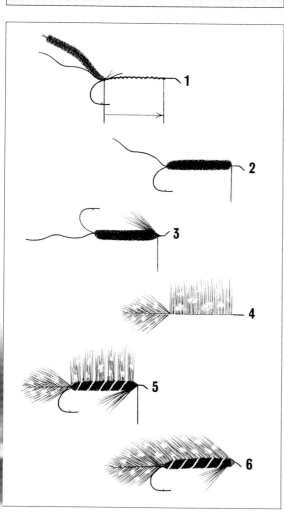

Tying Operations

1 Wind on the thread from behind the eye to above the barb and tie in the chenille and oval silver tinsel. Then wind the thread back in close turns to *at least* 3mm ($\frac{1}{8}$in) from the eye.

2 Wind on the chenille to form the body and tie off leaving room for the beard hackle and wing. Remove surplus chenille.

3 Turn the hook upside down in the vice. Tear out a bunch of fibres of appropriate length from a scarlet hackle and tie these in as shown.

4 Prepare the white/brown hen pheasant flank feathers one or two left, one or two right, so that each results as illustration 4.

5 Turn the hook right way up in the vice. Tie in the hen pheasant flank feathers back to back at the head with the stripped side of the quills lying over the hook shank. Then wind the tinsel through the fibres and over the hook shank, parting the fibres with a dubbing needle as you go to prevent them from being caught and flattened. Tie off at the eye end and remove any surplus tinsel and hackle butt ends.

6 Slope fibres towards the tail, wind a neat head, whip finish, trim out the thread and varnish the whip.

Variant	Chenille	Hackles
1	Fluorescent lime-green	White
2	White	Badger, natural or dyed red or hot orange
3	Red	Black
4	White	Rabbit strip, of any colour, as used in the Zowie, to replace the hackles

13 *Hammerhead* (Freddie Rice)

MATERIALS

Hook	Partridge code D4A, long shank, down eye, size 6, 8 or 10
Thread	Black
Underbody	Floss to match body cover
Body cover	Mylar piping – pearly, orange, gold or silver
Weighted head	Brass (for Golden) or lead, dumbell
Thorax	Fluorescent red, orange or lime-green wool
Overbody & tail	Black, olive or orange marabou plume
Head	Black

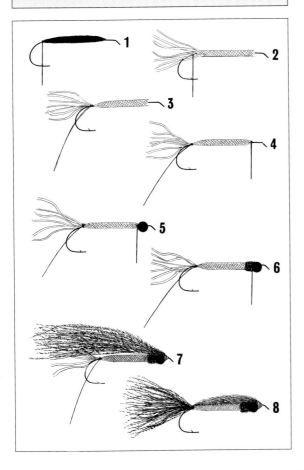

Tying Operations

1 Secure the thread above the barb, then tie in a 30cm (12in) length of floss and wind it back and forth forming the underbody to the shape shown. Tie off at the bend and trim excess floss.

2 Cut mylar tubing 12mm ($\frac{1}{2}$in) to 18mm ($\frac{3}{4}$in) longer than the floss body, extract the core and ease the tube over the eye and down to the bend. Tease out the ends of the mylar and press the tube further down the body to allow the ends to form a tail.

3 Use the thread to secure the mylar tubing to the shank ending with a whip finish. Then trim the thread to leave 30cm (12in) hanging at the joint.

4 Pull the mylar tightly forward over the eye, retie the thread over it and secure the mylar in place leaving room to fit the dumbells. Trim any mylar ends at the eye.

5 Depending upon the weight of fly sought, tie in a pair of small or medium dumbells a little way behind the eye and *under* the shank and secure them in place squarely, using a figure-of-eight tying.

6 Tie in, behind the dumbells, 7.5cm (3in) of wool which you should then wind on to form the thorax. Tie off and trim out the waste end of wool.

7 Cut a good swathe of marabou plume, wet and roll the cut ends, and tie this in on the eye side of the dumbells so that the uncut ends extend about 25mm (1in) beyond the bend. Trim marabou ends over the eye, wind a neat head ending with a whip finish. Trim out the thread at the eye and varnish the whip sparingly.

8 Pull the marabou down over the body and secure it above the barb with the length of thread hanging there. Whip finish and trim out the thread end.

11 *Goldie*

12 *Grey and Red Matuka*

13 *Hammerhead*

14 *Jack Frost* (Bob Church)

MATERIALS

Hook	Partridge code H1A, long shank, down eye, size 6, 8 or 10
Thread	White
Tail	Red wool
Body	White fluorescent wool
Overbody	Pre-stretched clear polythene strip 4mm ($\frac{3}{16}$in) wide
Wing	White marabou herls – a generous spray
Inner hackle	Scarlet, cock
Outer hackle	White, cock

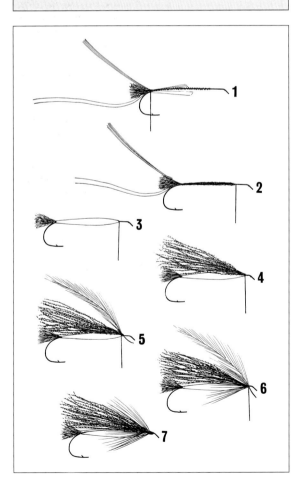

Tying Operations

1 Wind the thread from behind the eye to the start of the bend, at which point tie in the tail wool, the polythene strip and a length of floss.

2 Wind the thread back to behind the eye covering the ends of floss, polythene and tail fibres.

3 Wind on the floss, keeping it well spread and forming a sleek, shaped body, to a little short of the eye. Tie off and trim out the surplus floss. Next, wind on the polythene strip neatly covering the floss. Tie off behind the eye and trim surplus.

4 Tear or cut out a bunch of marabou herls, damp the tying-in end, roll that end to flatten the fibres and then tie them in to extend to the tip of the tail. Trim any tying-in ends at the eye.

5 Tie in the red cock hackle at the eye end of the body.

6 Lift the hackle to the vertical and wind two turns. Tie off, trim out the hackle butt and tip. Now tie in the white hackle in similar fashion.

7 Wind on the white hackle three turns, tie off and trim out the hackle butt and tip. Wind a neat head finishing with a whip finish, trim thread and varnish. When dry, compress the hackle fibres so that they are close to the body.

15 *Jersey Herd* *(Tom Ivens)*

MATERIALS

Hook	Partridge code D4A, long shank, down eye, size 6, 8 or 10
Thread	Black
Underbody	White floss (some prefer wool)
Body cover	Wide copper-coloured tinsel or, as in the original, a strip of Jersey milk cap foil
Tail and overbody	Eight to twelve strands of bronze peacock herl
Hackle	Cock hackle dyed hot orange
Head	Peacock herl, twisted into a rope

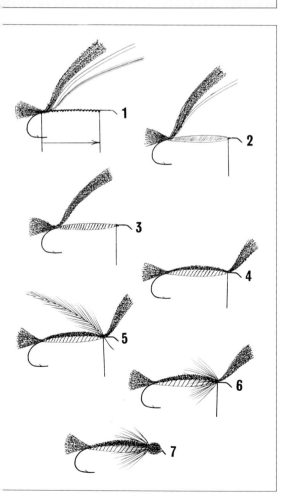

Tying Operations

1 Wind on the thread from a little behind the eye to above the barb and tie in the peacock herls, leaving 6mm (¼in) projecting for the tail, followed by the tinsel, then the floss or wool. Then wind the thread back to 6mm (¼in) from the eye.

2 Wind on the floss or wool, thickening at the centre until the thread is reached. Tie off and trim out excess floss or wool.

3 Varnish the underbody and, whilst it is still tacky, wind on the tinsel tightly, leaving no gaps, until the thread is reached. Tie off and trim out excess tinsel.

4 Coat the upper edge of the tinsel body with varnish and, whilst it is still tacky, pull the peacock herls forward and down to the eye where they are tied off, but *do not* remove the surplus herl ends – they will be needed for the head.

5 Select and tie in a doubled short-fibred cock hackle at the eye end of the body.

6 Wind on the doubled hackle two turns, tie off and trim out excess tip and butt ends.

7 Twist the peacock herl ends together at the eye in an anti-clockwise direction (clockwise for left-handers) and take two turns in front of the hackle to form a bold head. Tie off, trim any excess herl ends, wind a neat head ending with a whip finish and trim out the thread. Varnish the whipping.

Lead wire can be added in **1** before winding on the floss body. When the lead is wound, varnish it.

For the full description of the birth of this fly, see pages 56–58 of *Stillwater Fly-Fishing* by its originator Tom C. Ivens. The original fly sent by him to Farlow's and given to me by Mr. Woodcock of that company in 1970 is shown with its modern counterpart in the photograph.

The single layer of tinsel leaves somthing to be desired: I would prefer to tie it in behind the eye in **1** and wind it down to the tail and back again for better coverage.

16 *Muddler Minnow* (*Don Gapen*)

MATERIALS

Hook	Partridge code D4A, long shank, down eye, size 4, 6, 8 or 10
Thread	Brown
Tail	Folded slip of oak turkey wing fibres
Body	Flat gold tinsel, medium width
Wing	Sandwich of oak turkey/grey squirrel/oak turkey
Hackle	Deer hair body fibres
Head	Deer hair fibres 'spun' on and clipped to shape

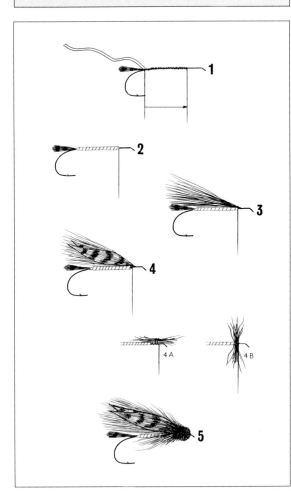

Tying Operations

1 Wind the thread from the eye to the bend, then add a folded slip of oak turkey wing quill for the tail of a size appropriate to the size of the hook, and the flat gold tinsel. Then wind the thread to within 8mm ($\frac{5}{16}$in) of the eye.

2 Wind on the tinsel in tight touching turns to 8mm ($\frac{5}{16}$in) from the eye and tie off.

3 Select and tie in, at the point where the thread hangs, a bunch of fibres from a grey squirrel tail to reach a little beyond the hook bend as shown. Secure them with turns of thread and trim waste ends.

4 Select a left and a right slip from an oak turkey wing quill and tie these in, one on either side of the squirrel fibres, length as illustration. Some prefer a shorter wing.

4A Select a small bunch of natural deer body hairs and take two slack turns round these and the hook shank as in illustration 4A. Pulling the thread and assisting the operation with the finger will result in these hairs spinning round the shank as in illustration 4B. A number (six to eight) of such spinnings are necessary, each being pressed against the first, for which an empty ball pen case is ideal.

5 When the spinnings are on, clip the front hair to a round ball shape as shown, leaving a few long hairs pointing to the rear as in illustration 5. Whip finish, trim the thread and varnish the whip.

Variation

Using fine nylon tubing (Saville's) a 'Muddler Head' can be spun on as in 4A and 4B. Such heads can then be slipped over the leader and pulled down to form a 'Muddler Head' to any lure. Try it!

14 *Jack Frost*

15 *Jersey Herd*

16 *Muddler Minnow*

17 *Nakkawakka* *(Freddie Rice)*

MATERIALS

Hook	Partridge code D4A, long shank, down eye, size 6, 8 or 10
Thread	Black
Tail	A spray of turkey marabou fibres, see table for colours
Body	Chenille, see table for colours
Rear wing overlay	A spray of turkey marabou fibres, see table for colours
Front wing overlay	A spray of turkey marabou fibres, see table for colours
Head weight	Fine lead wire
Head	Chenille, see table for colours

Tying Operations

1 Wind on the thread in close turns from the eye to the start of the bend, at which point tie in the tail (to extend a hook length beyond bend) and the body chenille. Then wind the thread to the point indicated.

2 Varnish the turns of thread then wind on the chenille in close turns to where the thread hangs. Secure the chenille there leaving the balance for use in **4**.

3 Tie in the rear wing overlay to extend half-way to tail tip. Then wind the thread to next point indicated.

4 Varnish the turns of thread and wind on the balance of the chenille to where the thread hangs. Tie off and trim surplus chenille.

5 Tie in the front wing overlay to reach just beyond the hook bend and secure.

6 Tie in 5cm (2in) of chenille for the head, and then the lead wire. Then wind the thread to just short of the eye.

7 Wind on the lead wire in three reducing layers to form a hump at the head which is then varnished.

8 Wind on the chenille head, whip finish, trim the chenille and thread and varnish the whip.

9 When wet the fly appears thus. A 6lb (2.7kg) (minimum) leader is needed to fish the fly, sink and draw, and to hop the lake bed, as indicated in 'A' to 'A'. Developed in the early 1970s this fly was then pre-Dog Nobbler and bore the name 'Bedhopper'.

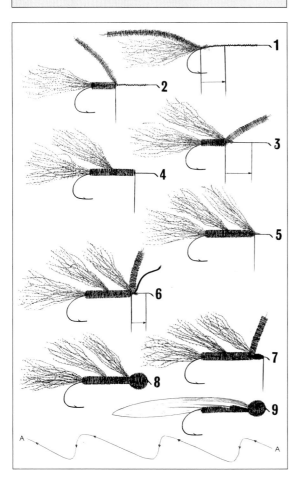

Tail	Body	Rear Overlay	Front Overlay	Head
White	White	White	Olive	White
White	Grey	Black	Orange	White
Black	Scarlet	White	White	Black
Orange	White	Orange	Black	White

18 *Orange Crystal* (*Freddie Rice*)

MATERIALS

Hook	Partridge code D4A long shank, down eye for bottom work or code H1A long shank, down eye for mid and upper levels, both size 10
Thread	Orange
Tail	Lureflash Crystal Hair, hot orange, ref. CH8
Body	As tail
Hackle	Hot orange, cock
Head	Orange thread

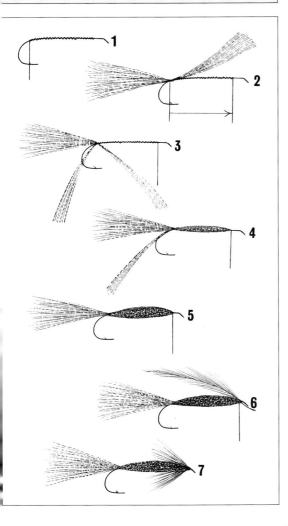

Tying Operations (colour plate on cover)

1 Wind the thread from 4mm ($\frac{3}{16}$in) from the eye to above the barb.

2 Crystal Hair is supplied as a folded hank. Cut approximately 35 fibres at the fold. Tie in the Crystal Hair so that a full shank length overhangs the bend. This hair is slippery so a secure, varnished joint is necessary.

3 When the varnished joint is dry, divide the hair into two equal bunches with a dubbing needle. Beginning at the tail joint to ensure a clean separation, clip the left-hand bunch into hackle pliers and lay it out of the way to the left.

4 Wind on the right-hand bunch tightly (over a varnished layer of thread) moving to the right. Form a carrot shape with this action and progress to where the thread hangs. Then use the thread to secure the hair in place. Trim the excess.

5 Pick up the left-hand bunch of hair and wind this flatly and tightly over the first layer, ending slightly beyond the joint securing the first bunch. Tie off securely and trim the excess. Now varnish the body in two good coats and leave to dry thoroughly by hanging up by the point. Then produce two other copies exactly as before – it is never good to tie one only.

6 When the varnished body is thoroughly dry, select a hackle about 6.5cm (2½in) long, strip out the fluffy base fibres and tie it in behind the eye.

7 Now double the hackle (see page 9) and wind it on three or four turns. Tie off, trim out hackle tip and butt end, wind a neat head ending with a whip finish and trim out the thread. Finally, varnish the whip. This very durable fly produces good catches particularly in early or late season or during the summer when there is a good 'chop' on the water.

Body and tail (Crystal Hair)	Hackle
Mother of pearl (ref. CH14)	Black or dark green
Peacock (ref. CH1)	Hot orange or white
Hot yellow (ref. CH11)	Black

19 *Polystickle* (Richard Walker)

MATERIALS

Hook	Partridge code D4A, long shank, down eye, size 6 or 8 (8 most popular)
Thread	Black
Underbody	Flat silver tinsel
Gut	Fluorescent (or normal) scarlet floss or wool
Body cover	Prestretched polythene strip 5–6mm ($\frac{1}{4}$in) wide
Tail and back	Raffene strip 5mm ($\frac{3}{16}$in) wide, wet and pulled tightly to eye – brown, brown-olive, buff, yellow, orange, green, green-olive, at your choice
Throat	Either a slip of scarlet wool or floss, or scarlet hackle fibres tied underneath as a beard or false hackle
Head	Working thread wound on to form a substantial head

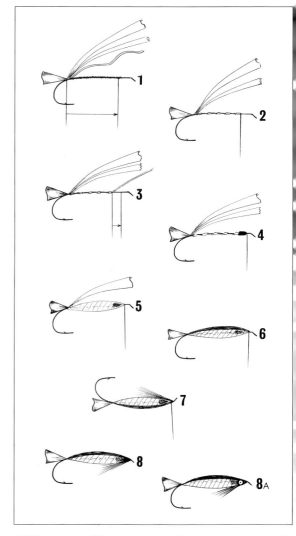

Tying Operations

1 Wind on tight turns of thread from the eye to the bend and then tie in the underbody tinsel, polythene body cover strip and Raffene for tail/back so that approximately 6mm ($\frac{1}{4}$in) extends over the bend. Then wind the thread over two-thirds of the shank towards the eye.

2 Wind on the tinsel in widely spaced turns to where the thread hangs. Tie off and remove surplus tinsel.

3 Tie in the floss for the gut, then wind the thread to 3mm ($\frac{1}{8}$in) from the eye.

4 Wind on the floss forming the gut, tying off at 3mm ($\frac{1}{8}$in) from the eye. Trim waste.

5 Wind on the stretched polythene tightly to and fro forming the body shape ending at the point where the thread hangs. Tie off and remove surplus polythene. Varnish the body in two coats.

6 Wet the Raffene, pull this tightly over the body to the eye and tie in. Remove surplus Raffene at the eye.

7 Tie in the throat material (I prefer the scarlet hackle fibres) turning the hook upside down in the vice if this eases the operation. Trim off any surplus extending over the eye.

8 Using your thread, wind on a substantial head as shown, finishing with a neat whip finish. Trim out the thread and varnish the head. An eye can be added on each side of the head, but this is optional (illustration 8A).

17 *Nakkawakka*

19 *Polystickle*

20 *Soft Touch*

20 *Soft Touch* (*Freddie Rice*)

MATERIALS

Hook	Partridge code H1A or D4A, long shank, down eye, size 8 or 10
Thread	Black
Tail and body	Black, white, olive, orange or red marabou plume
Overlay	Black, white, red, green or yellow plastazote, 3mm (⅛in) thick
Hot spot (optional)	Fluorescent red, orange, or lime-green wool
Head	Black

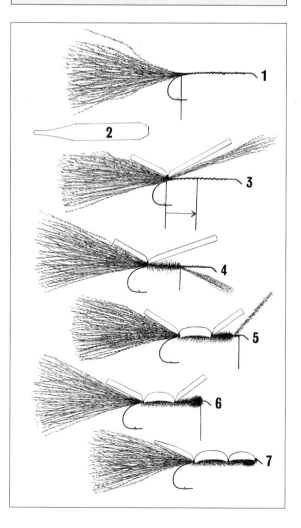

Tying Operations

1 Wind the thread from behind the eye to above the barb. Cut a good swathe of marabou plume, wet the cut ends, roll them and tie them in to reach a hook length beyond the bend. Trim out waste ends.

2 Cut a piece of plastazote approximately 25mm (1in) long for size 10 or 30mm (1¼in) long for size 8 and shape it as shown.

3 Place the shaped plastazote over the shank so that the blunt end is just beyond the eye, and use the thread to tie it down above the barb. Next, cut a much smaller swathe of marabou and tie this in at the same point. Wind the thread half-way along the shank.

4 Wind on the small swathe of marabou forming the rear portion of the body and secure it where the thread hangs. Leave the remainder of the marabou hanging.

5 Pull the right leg of plastazote down over the shank and bind it down then wind the thread to a little short of the eye. Wind on the remaining marabou to where the thread hangs. Tie off and trim out waste. Then, as an option, tie in 5cm (2in) of fluorescent wool for the hot spot.

6 If the wool has been added, wind it on forming a narrow band. Tie off and trim excess wool.

7 Pull the remaining end of plastazote down and secure it behind the eye. Trim out any excess, add a neat head ending with a whip finish. Trim out the thread and varnish the head.

Using the Fly

This fly can be used as a lure or as a nymph. Using a fast sinking line, and letting it settle, the fly will lift and either an intermittent pull will draw it down as a lure, or a steady, slow retrieve will give the impression of a nymph. It is best to tie the latter with olive marabou and green plastazote.

21 *Special Baby Doll* (*Sid Brock*)

MATERIALS

Hook	Partridge code D4A, long shank, down eye, size 6, 8 or 10
Thread	Black
Underbody	Black wool or floss
Body cover	Black plastic tape or strips of black, pre-stretched refuse bag, 5mm ($\frac{3}{16}$in) wide
Gut	Red wool, plain or fluorescent
Tail and back	Signal green fluorescent wool or tow wool
Head	Built up with turns of thread

Tying Operations

1 Wind the thread from behind the eye to above the barb where the wool/floss for the underbody is tied in.

2 Wind the wool/floss back and forth forming the underbody (shaped as illustration 2) ending up above the barb where it is tied off and the excess trimmed out.

3 Tie in a fair length of pre-stretched black polythene (such as refuse bag) followed by the fluorescent wool for the tail and back. Then wind the thread to the eye end of the body.

4 Wind on the black polythene strip, overlapping each turn a little, to the front of the body. Tie off and trim excess polythene. That done, tie in the wool for the gut at the eye end of the body. Wind the thread to behind the eye.

5 Wind on the wool in a narrow band leaving room to wind an enlarged head of thread later. Tie off and trim out excess wool. Then pull the green fluorescent wool, forming the back, down over the body and gut where it is tied down and any excess trimmed.

6 Finally, wind an enlarged head with the thread ending with a whip finish. Trim out the thread and varnish the head in four coats. If desired, you can add a white eye with a black centre when the varnish is dry.

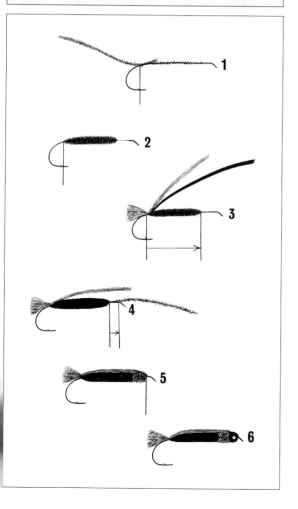

22 *Viva Lure* (Victor Furze)

MATERIALS

Hook	Partridge code D4A, long shank, down eye, size 6, 8 or 10
Thread	Black
Tail	Fluorescent lime-green tow wool
Body	Black chenille
Body rib	Flat silver tinsel or silver wire
Beard hackle	Black cock
Wing	Black turkey marabou plume

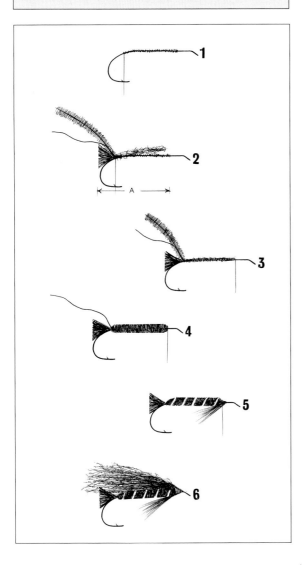

Tying Operations

1 From well behind the eye wind on the thread in close, tight turns to above the barb.

2 Cut a length of tow wool as long as distance 'A' shown and tie this in to leave 6mm (¼in) beyond the point of tying in. Tie in a short length of tinsel or wire and approximately 10cm (4in) of chenille from which 6mm (¼in) of 'fur' has first been stripped from the end to be tied in.

3 Wind the thread back to where you started in 1 above, binding down *only* the wool lying over the shank.

4 Varnish the wool on the hook shank then wind on the chenille in close, tight turns clockwise to where the thread hangs. Tie off and trim out the surplus chenille.

5 Pick up the tinsel or wire and wind it over the chenille in four to six open anti-clockwise turns depending on the hook size used. Tie off and trim the excess tinsel or wire. Tear or cut a bunch of fibres from a large black hackle and tie these in at the eye end of the body so that the points reach halfway to the hook point. Trim any waste ends.

6 Tear or cut 36mm (1½in) from the fibres covering one side of the marabou plume, adjust them against the hook so that the fine tips extend just beyond the end of the tail, wet the excess (which will extend beyond the eye) and twist it into a rope. Keeping the same adjustment, tie in the marabou ensuring that it lies *on top* of the shank for it has a tendency to follow the pull of the thread and will, unless watched, drift to the far side of the shank. When several securing turns have been wound on, trim the excess marabou fibres cleanly just behind the eye then wind a neat head ending with a whip finish. Trim off the thread and varnish the head.

The original had a tail of fluorescent green, wide tinsel rib and a wing of goat hair and marabou plume mixed. There are other variations. I change the green tail to one of 'Glow Ball' whilst another variant has the tow wool wound in front of a shortened body. All three types are shown in the photograph.

21 *Special Baby Doll*

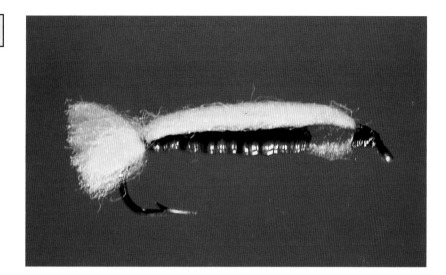

22 *Viva Lure*

23 *Whisky Fly*

23 *Whisky Fly* *(Albert Willock)* *(Updated)*

MATERIALS

Hook	Partridge code D4A or H1A, long shank, down eye, size 8 or 10
Thread	Scarlet
Tag	Scarlet fluorescent floss
Body	Floss, as tag
Body rib	Flat gold or silver tinsel, or Mylar medium width
Wing	Hot orange, preferably of calftail, but bucktail or bleached and dyed squirrel tail otherwise
Head hackle	Hot orange, cock
Elongated head	Floss, as tag

Tying Operations

1 Secure the thread behind the eye then wind it in close turns to a point above the barb. Do not let it progress round the bend.

2 Cut and tie in about 30cm (12in) of fluorescent scarlet floss where the thread hangs, the waste end to point towards the eye.

3 Wind the tying thread towards the eye in five close turns, then wind on the floss flatly to where the thread hangs. Secure the floss with two turns of thread but do not trim the remainder of the floss.

4 Cut 7.5cm (3in) of tinsel, trim one end to an angled point and tie it in underneath the hook on the eye side of the tag. That done, wind the tying thread to point 'A'.

5 Pick up and wind on the floss flatly forming a slim body to point 'A'. Secure the floss there but do not trim the remainder of the floss.

6 Pick up and wind on the tinsel in five tight but open turns to point 'A'. Secure it there and trim out surplus tinsel only.

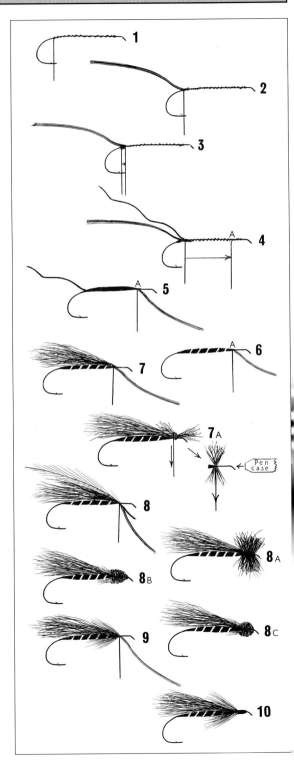

7 Cut a small bunch of hair, of the type you prefer, to reach from the eye end of the body to 6mm (¼in) beyond the outside bend of the hook. Lay this bunch on top of the shank then, using the pinch and loop method, secure the cut ends with several tight turns of tying thread. That done, trim any waste ends and add a droplet of varnish to these securing turns.

8 Select a hot orange cock hackle about 5cm (2in) in length and tie this in securely at the eye end of the body to lie flatly over the hook shank, concave side uppermost.

9 Lift the hackle to the vertical then wind it on four turns keeping the floss just to the right of those turns. Secure the hackle with three turns of thread and trim out the tip and butt end of the hackle.

10 Wind the thread to just behind the hook eye leaving the floss hanging at 'A'. Then pick up the floss and wind it back and forth from the eye side of the hackle to just behind the eye building up an elongated head ending up close behind the eye. Secure the floss in that position and trim out the waste end of floss. Add a whip finish with the thread which is then also trimmed off. Finally, varnish just the head in three coats and allow it to dry well.

The Whisky Muddler (an alternative)

To tie the Muddler version, first separate the outer case from the case of a ball-point pen for use later. Tie the Whisky Fly as 1 to 7 above then proceed as follows:

7A With the thread positioned immediately on the eye side of the wing ends, cut a small bunch of deer body hair and, with this laid horizontally over the shank at that point, take two *loose* turns of thread round the hair and hook shank. Pulling the thread firmly down vertically will cause the hair to flare somewhat like a hackle. Take one turn of thread round the hook shank alone then use the smaller opening in the empty ball pen case, pushed over the hook eye and hook shank, to press the flared hair back against the wing tyings.

8A Repeat the process of cutting, tying-in, flaring, securing and packing back the hair until all the space between wing ends and hook eye is tightly filled with flared hair. This may take up to seven or eight bunches of hair to produce. When complete, whip finish and trim out the thread. The miniature porcupine of hair can then be trimmed with sharp scissors to a bullet shape as in illustration 8B or a ball as in 8C. You may like to leave a few of the deer hairs nearest the wing projecting to the rear as in the usual dressing of the Muddler Minnow. Leave varnishing the whip finish until the head has been trimmed to shape.

24 *Zowie* (*Freddie Rice*)

MATERIALS

Hook	Partridge code D4A, long shank, down eye, size 6 or 8
Weight	(Optional) Fine lead wire
Thread	To match body colour
Tail	(Optional) Fluorescent lime green, hot orange, red wool or Fireball Fluff
Body	Chenille, white, black, orange or olive
Rib	Fine oval tinsel, silver or gold
Wing	Hair strip, white, brown, orange or black rabbit, mink or similar, cured hide
Head hackle	(Optional) Black, orange, red or olive, cock
Hot spot head	(Optional) As tail

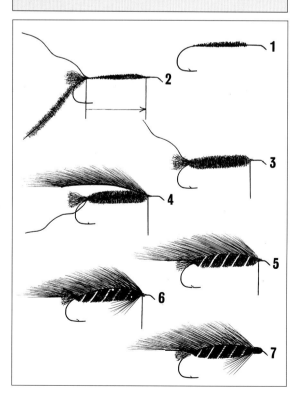

Tying Operations

1 For a leaded type, wind on lead wire over the level shank in one or two layers, a little short of both eye and bend.

2 Wind on the thread from behind the eye to the start of the bend binding down the lead, then cut the tail wool and tie this in to extend 5–8mm ($\frac{3}{16}$–$\frac{5}{16}$in) beyond the bend. Next, strip 6mm ($\frac{1}{4}$in) from the end of a 10cm (4in) length of chenille and tie in the stripped end level with the tail joint. Follow this with 10cm (4in) of oval tinsel at the same spot and wind the thread back to 5mm ($\frac{3}{16}$in) from the eye.

3 Wind on the chenille in close turns to where the thread hangs. Tie off and trim excess chenille.

4 Cut the hair wing strip 3mm ($\frac{1}{8}$in) wide from the skin side of a rabbit, mink, etc., hide with a scalpel trying to ensure an even width. It can be body length or longer at your whim. Cut the fur from 2mm ($\frac{1}{16}$in) of the front end, trim its width to a blunt point and tie in this point securely behind the eye keeping it on top of the shank.

5 Next, using a dubbing needle, part the fur above the tail joint and take the tinsel through the gap at an angle to move forward. Repeat the parting of the fur and the winding of the tinsel every 3mm ($\frac{1}{8}$in) until the eye end of the body is reached where the tinsel is tied off and the waste end trimmed out.

6 If a hackle is included, use a largish saddle hackle, strip out the fluffy base fibres and tie it in behind the eye. Wind on two or three turns, tie off and trim the hackle tip and butt end.

7 If a 'hot spot' head is desired, tie in a short length of the chosen material, wind a narrow band, tie off and trim out excess. Add a four or five turn whip finish to a wound head which you should varnish after trimming out the thread.

King Zowie

The wing is white Arctic Fox which needs a heavily leaded body to overcome the air in the thick underfur. Good on the dam wall!

24 Zowie

25 Balloon Caddis

26 Booby

Nymphs

25 Balloon Caddis – Emerging pupa
(Roman Moser)

MATERIALS

Hook	Partridge, code CS2, barbless, size 10, 12 or 14
Thread	Yellow or primrose
Balloon	5mm ($\frac{3}{16}$in) wide plastazote strip, yellow, 3mm ($\frac{1}{8}$in) thick
Body	Polyproxseal dubbing, pale olive
Wing	Brown deer body hair

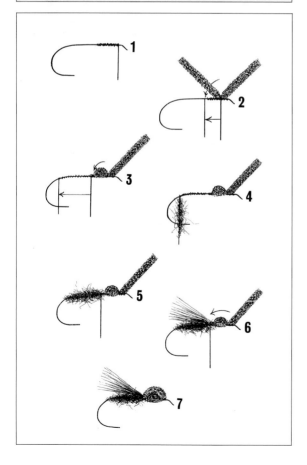

Tying Operations

1 Wind on a short bed of thread behind the eye.

2 Cut a 5mm ($\frac{3}{16}$in) wide strip of yellow plastazote. Tie this in by its centre behind the eye then jump the thread 4mm ($\frac{3}{16}$in) towards the bend where the left leg of the plastazote is tied down forming the balloon hump. Trim the remainder of that plastasote leg leaving only the hump.

3 Wind the thread to above the barb.

4 Dub the polyproxseal on to the thread.

5 Wind on the dubbed polyproxseal in close turns to behind the balloon hump.

6 Cut a reasonable bunch of brown deer hairs of a length to reach from behind the hump to the outside hook bend. Tie them in so that the cut ends are immediately behind the balloon hump and sitting on top of the hook.

7 Pull the second leg of plastazote back over the existing hump and tie it down there. Trim out excess plastazote, add a whip finish, trim out the thread and varnish the whip.

Roman Moser has said that if he could have only one fly, this would be it.

26 *Booby* (*Gordon Fraser*)

MATERIALS

Hook	Partridge code H1A, Capt. Hamilton nymph hook size 10 or 12
Thread	To match body colour
Buoyant head	Two ethofoam balls 5mm ($\frac{3}{16}$in) in size enclosed in nylon stocking
Tail	Hackle fibres or marabou tufts to match body colour
Body	Yellow, olive, black or claret seal fur or a blend
Rib	Gold or silver wire, oval gold tinsel or monofilament
Thorax	(Optional) Light coloured hare body fur or similar

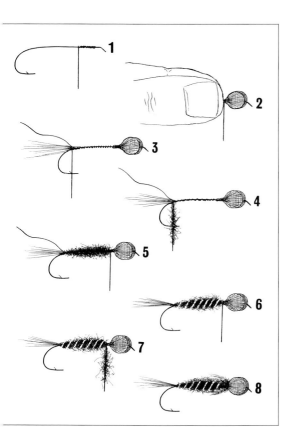

The use of an ethofoam ball enclosed in nylon stocking material was initiated by an American, Charles E. Brookes, and used by John Goddard and Brian Clarke for their Suspender Nymph. This has now been converted for use on a fast sinking line by Gordon Fraser, resulting in a very successful pattern. In Fraser's fly two ethofoam balls are enclosed side by side in nylon stocking and then secured to the hook to sit either side of and just behind the hook eye.

Tying Operations

1 Lay on two layers of thread behind the eye.

2 Enclose two ethofoam balls, each approximately 5mm ($\frac{3}{16}$in), side by side within a piece of tightly stretched white or very pale nylon stocking leaving enough to facilitate the closing end to be secured to the hook shank lying back toward the bend. Set the enclosed balls in place on top of the hook and neatly secure the closing end to the shank. That done, use figure-of-eight tyings round and between the balls to add security, then remove surplus nylon.

3 Run the thread to above the barb where the selected form of tail is tied in followed by 7.5cm (3in) of ribbing.

4 Dub on the seal fur ready for winding.

5 Wind on the dubbed fur to a little short of the balls, then leave the thread hanging.

6 Wind on the ribbing five to seven turns to where the thread hangs which you should then use to secure the ribbing. Trim any excess.

7 For a thorax dub a little fur on to the thread.

8 Wind a narrow band of fur and tie off. Finally, whip finish and trim out the thread. *Do not apply cellulose varnish to the whip* if you use polystyrene balls instead of ethofoam because they will disintegrate.

Fraser's earlier fly was the reverse of the Dog Nobbler, the ethofoam balls making it float off the bottom. This version can be tied with the materials as for the Nobbler but with the nylon enclosed balls instead of a split shot.

27 *Bright Eye Nymph* (*Freddie Rice*)

MATERIALS

Hook	Partridge code A, standard shank, size 10, 12 or 14
Thread	To match body colour
Tail	Cock hackle fibres – see table for colours
Body	Seal fur, Antron or similar – see table for colours
Hackle	Cock – see table for colours
Bright eye	Flat pearl, or flat or embossed gold or silver tinsel
Head:	Thread, to match body colour

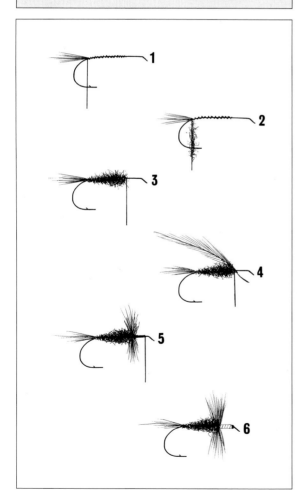

Tying Operations

1 Wind the thread from the centre of the shank to above the barb where the tail fibres are tied in with the points extending two-thirds of the shank length beyond the tying-in point.

2 Dub on the body material sparsely ready for winding on.

3 Wind on the dubbing over two-thirds of shank length and remove any excess dubbing from the thread.

4 Tie in the hackle to lie flat over the shank.

5 Lift the hackle to the vertical and wind it on in three close turns. Tie off and trim hackle tip and butt end, then wind the thread in close touching turns to behind the eye to provide a smooth base for the tinsel windings.

6 Immediately behind the eye tie in the tinsel then wind it in close turns up to the hackle and back again to behind the eye. Tie off, trim out excess tinsel and wind a neat head ending with a whip finish. Then trim out the thread and varnish the head and the bright eye.

This is a good top and/or middle dropper fly or a team of three. Ringing the colour changes pays dividends (see below).

Hackle	Tail	Body	Bright Eye Tinsel
Black	Black	Black	Silver, gold or pearl
Badger	Badger	Fiery brown	Gold
Claret	Postal red	Claret	Silver, gold or pearl
Black	G.P. tippet	Orange	Pearl
Badger	Badger	Grey	Silver
Grizzle	Olive	Olive	Gold

27 *Bright Eye Nymph*

28 *Corixa*

29 *Damsel Nymph*

28 *Corixa* *(Gordon Fraser)*

MATERIALS

Hook	Down eye Sproat type, size 12
Thread	Fawn or beige
Lead underbody	(Optional) Wine bottle lead, wound on in strips or bound on flat
Wing case	Hen pheasant tail fibres
Overbody	Pale yellow rayon floss (white as an option)

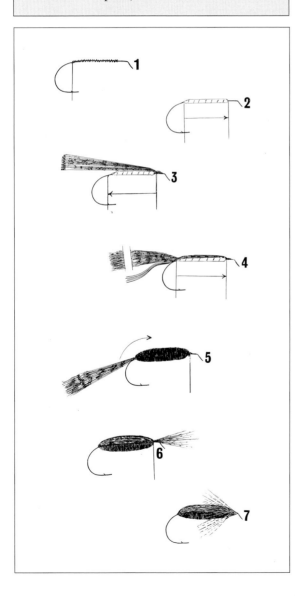

Tying Operations

1 Wind the thread from a little behind the eye to the start of the hook bend.

2 Lay on the fine lead strip/s and then bind them down on top of the shank, *or* wind on the strip to a little behind the eye and then bind the thread over it to the eye. Either way, varnish the underbody.

3 Cut a dozen or so pheasant fibres from the quill and tie in the butt ends a little behind the eye, the long ends to extend beyond the bend. Wind the thread over them to the start of the bend.

4 At the bend, tie in a length of rayon floss, then wind the thread back to behind the eye.

5 Wind on the rayon floss to form a maggot shaped body. Tie off and trim excess floss.

6 Pull the pheasant fibres over the body tightly and tie them down at the eye.

7 Split the pheasant fibre tips into two bunches and bind them down one bunch on each side of the body. Form a neat head, whip finish, trim out the thread and varnish the head.

Using the Fly

Knowing Gordon's use of this fly may be helpful. In early season a single leaded fly fished deep is used. Later Gordon fishes in shallow water, calm weedy bays and where old ditches exist. A lightly leaded fly is cast out, allowed to sink but kept in touch. When deep enough he uses figure-of-eight to draw a 2ft line fairly quickly, then pauses to let the fly sink again – the corixa habit. Otherwise he uses two unleaded flies, and an unretrieved floating line, and lets them drift.

29 *Damsel Nymph* *(Freddie Rice)*

MATERIALS

Hook	Partridge code H1A, long shank, size 10 or 12
Thread	Olive
Tail	Three small olive hackle tips
Body	Medium olive seal fur
Body rib	Oval, or fine flat, gold tinsel
Hackle	Brown or grey partridge
Thorax	Dark olive or fiery brown seal fur

Tying Operations

1 Wind on the thread from behind the eye to the start of the hook bend. Lead can then be added in area X.

2 Tie in the hackle tips so that they extend 7mm ($\frac{1}{4}$in) beyond the end of the body.

3 Tie in the tinsel at the tail joint, then wax the thread and dub on the body fur.

4 Wind on (anti-clockwise) the dubbed body fur to a carrot shape until 5mm ($\frac{3}{16}$in) from the eye.

5 Wind on the tinsel (clockwise) four or five turns forming the rib. Tie off and trim excess tinsel.

6 Prepare the partridge hackle (illustration 6A) pulling the fibres down from the short tip towards the butt end (illustration 6B).

7 Tie in the hackle by its tip leaving the rest overhanging the eye. Then dub on a small amount of seal fur ready to wind the thorax.

8 With the hackle still protruding, wind the thorax covering the hackle tip already tied in.

9 Clip hackle pliers to the hackle butt, lift the hackle to the vertical and wind on three turns. Tie off, trim excess hackle butt and wind a neat head ending with a whip finish. Trim out thread and varnish the whip.

10 The finished fly.

For a leaded version, wind on six to ten turns of fine lead wire over area 'X' as in illustration 1.

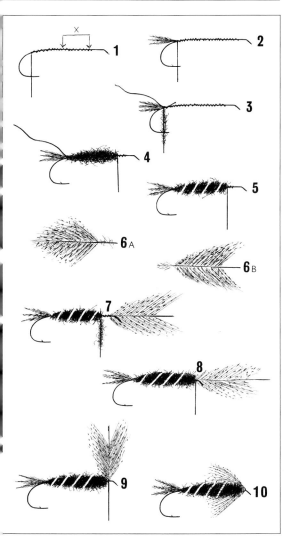

30 *Effingham Green Midge* *(John Hutton)*

MATERIALS

Hook	Partridge code K4A, grub shrimp hook, size 12 or 14
Thread	Primrose
Underbody	Signal green DRF Floss
Overbody	Ultrafine pale olive Swannandaze (No. 78)
Thorax	Light olive bug fur
Wing case	One fibre only, olive goose biot

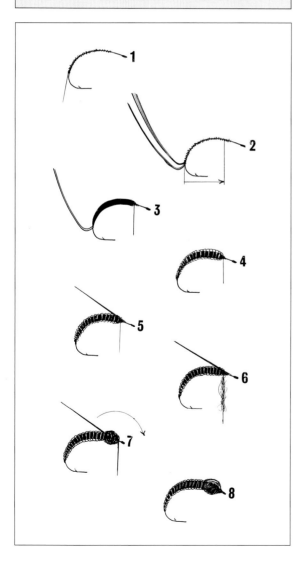

Tying Operations

1 Secure the thread on the shank well behind the eye and then wind it in close, even turns to the position round the bend indicated.

2 Tie in a length (approximately 15cm (6in)) of DRF floss and the Swannandaze, the tip of which has been slimmed down with scissors to avoid a bulky start. Wind the thread back to 3mm ($\frac{1}{8}$in) from the eye.

3 Wind on the DRF floss *flatly* to form a slim, tapered body ending where the thread hangs. Tie off and trim surplus floss.

4 Wind on the Swannandaze (the flat side inside, rounded side outside) over the DRF body in touching turns to where the thread hangs. Tie off and trim surplus Swannandaze.

5 Select a single slip of goose biot and tie this in by the thick end at the eye end of the body, so that the tapered end lies back over the already wound body.

6 Dub a small amount of bug fur thinly on to the thread.

7 Wind on the bug fur to give a not too bulky thorax. Remove any unused fur.

8 Pull the tapered end of the goose biot over the thorax and, ensuring that it sits wholly *over* the thorax, tie it down behind the eye. Closely trim off the tip of the biot, wind a neat head, whip finish, trim thread and varnish the head.

Using the Fly

The fly is fished very slowly (on a leader greased to within 30cm (1ft) of the fly) on a floating line. In Hampshire and other southern waters it is best used from late April or early May through to season end. A mid-May commencement is best on Midland and northern waters.

A goose biot is derived from those fibres forming the narrow side of a goose wing quill.

30 *Effingham Green Midge*

31 *Emerging Brown Sedge Pupa*

32 *Fraser Nymph*

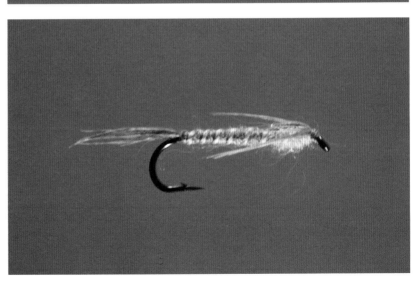

31 *Emerging Brown Sedge Pupa* (Freddie Rice)

MATERIALS

Hook	Partridge Caddis type, code K4A size 12 or 14
Thread	Brown
Tails	Fine tips of pheasant tail fibres used for body
Body	Four to six cock pheasant centre tail fibres
Body rib	Thin strip of brown plastic raffia
Wing stubs	Narrow slips of brownish-grey feather fibres
Legs	Use the body fibre ends bent back under the body
Horns	(Optional) Two fibres from a partridge back hackle

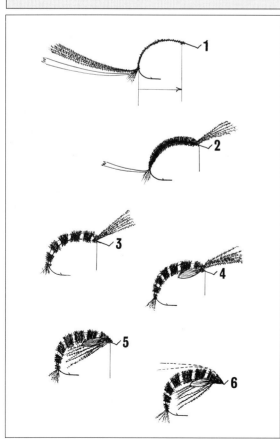

Tying Operations

1 Wind the thread from well behind the eye to well round the bend, as shown, at which point tie in the body fibres with short, fine tips protruding, followed by the raffia strip just over 2mm ($\frac{1}{16}$in) wide. Wind the thread back to where you started, thickening the body as you go.

2 Varnish the shank and, whilst it is still tacky, wind on the body fibres to where the thread hangs, where they are secured. Do not trim the excess.

3 Pick up the raffia, wet it and wind it tightly in open turns over the body (so that a series of pheasant fibres protrude) to where the thread hangs. Tie off and trim excess.

4 Cut the two slips for the wing stubs approximately 3mm ($\frac{1}{8}$in) wide and tie one in on each side of the body to project outwards slightly. Trim any excess.

5 Separate the excess body fibre ends in two bunches and bend one over the left, the other over the right side of the body and press them beneath the shank where they are then secured in position.

6 If adding horns, cut the two fibres from the partridge hackle and tie these in above the body and just behind the eye to lie over the upper body. Wind a neat head completing with a whip finish, trim out the thread and varnish the head.

Variations

There are two further variations of interest – a body of dark olive goose or swan herl with olive raffia rib, or a body of hot orange goose or swan herl with a pale buff raffia rib. Otherwise the tying for both is as indicated above.

32 *Fraser Nymph* (Gordon Fraser)

MATERIALS

Hook	Long shank, down eye, size 10, 12 or 14
Thread	Fawn
Rib	Fawn coloured domestic thread (such as Sylko)
Tail and abdomen	Twelve (for size 10) down to six (for size 14) hen pheasant tail fibres over two-thirds body length
Thorax case and legs	Hen pheasant tail fibres
Thorax	Creamy beige fur blend, one-third body length
Head	Fawn thread, well varnished

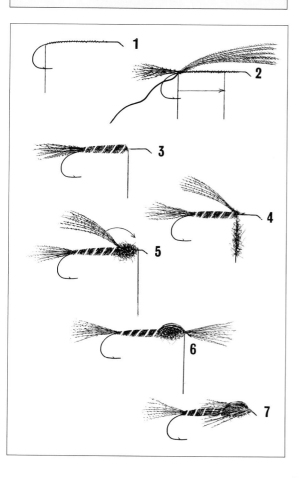

Tying Operations

Start by mentally dividing the level shank into three sections, two are for the abdomen, one for the thorax.

1 Secure the thread 3mm ($\frac{1}{8}$in) behind the eye, then wind it in close turns to above the barb.

2 Tie in a short length of ribbing thread and the appropriate number of pheasant tail fibres, the natural tips to overhang the outside hook bend by 6mm ($\frac{1}{4}$in). Then wind the thread neatly back over two-thirds of the shank.

3 Gather the pheasant tail fibres into a bunch and wind these on in close turns to where the thread hangs forming a slim body. Next, wind on the ribbing thread in five open turns. Tie off and trim out excess ends of pheasant tail and ribbing.

4 Cut approximately eight further pheasant tail fibres and tie these in so that the natural tips will reach the centre of the tail. *This length is import-ant.* Then dub the thorax fur slimly on to the thread.

5 Wind on the dubbed fur to a little short of the eye forming the shaped thorax. Remove any surplus dubbing from the thread.

6 Gather the pheasant tail fibres and pull these over the thorax where they are secured behind the eye with the fine points extending beyond.

7 Separate the pheasant tail fibres into two equal bunches and tie these back so that there is a bunch on each side of the thorax and slightly spread. Wind a neat head ending with a whip finish. Trim out the thread neatly and varnish the head.

Variation

This is an excellent pattern when olives are hatching or when fawn buzzers are appearing in numbers. An experiment I tried of changing the thorax to olive rabbit fur resulted in a passable damsel nymph when tied on a 10 or 12 hook.

33 *Free Living Caseless Caddis* (Roman Moser)

MATERIALS

Hook	Partridge code CS2O, barbless, size 12
Thread	Dark olive or brown
Weight	Fine lead wire wound over level shank area
Abdomen	Light olive elastic furry foam (Lureflash)
Thorax	Fur from hare's ear

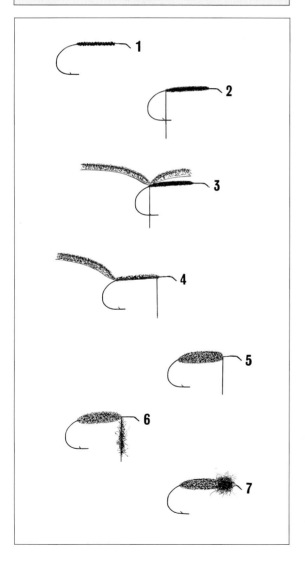

Tying Operations

1 Starting at least 3mm ($\frac{1}{8}$in) from the eye, wind on lead wire in close turns over the level area of the hook shank.

2 Secure the thread behind the eye then wind it back and forth securing the wire in place ending up at the start of the bend.

3 Cut a strip of furry foam 5mm ($\frac{3}{16}$in) wide and tie this in furry side uppermost with main strip extending to the left.

4 Wind the thread back to approximately 5mm ($\frac{3}{16}$in) from the eye tying down the short length of furry foam as you go.

5 Stretch and wind on the furry foam to where the thread hangs, keeping the furry not the foam side outside. Tie off and trim out surplus furry foam.

6 Pinch out the hair from the hare's ear (using the nails of the index finger and thumb) and dub this on to the thread ready for winding on.

7 Wind on the dubbed hair forming the thorax to just behind the eye. Remove any excess hair from the thread, wind a neat head ending with a whip finish. Trim out thread and varnish the whip.

**33 Free Living
Caseless Caddis**

34 Furry Foam Nymph

35 G.R.P. Nymph

34 *Furry Foam Nymph* *(Freddie Rice)*

MATERIALS

Hook	Partridge code H1A, long shank, size 10 or 12
Thread	Olive
Tail	Olive marabou plume and six to eight strands of orange Crystal Hair
Body and wing case	Olive furry foam, 3–4mm (⅛in) wide
Body rib	The same Crystal Hair as in tail
Hot spot thorax	Fluorescent orange Fireball Fluff or wool

Tying Operations

1 Wind the thread from behind the eye to above the barb where you should tie in a swathe of marabou plume for the tail, the strands of Crystal Hair and the furry foam, the end of which has been cut to a point. Then wind the thread back almost to where you started.

2 Wind on the furry foam, furry side outmost over two-thirds of the shank. Tie off but *do not* trim excess foam which should be left projecting upwards.

3 Twist the long strands of Crystal Hair into a tight rope then wind this on as a rib five turns. Tie off and trim excess hair ends. Next tie in the material for the hot spot thorax after which wind the thread to just short of the eye.

4 Wind on the hot spot material and form the thorax. Tie off and trim any waste ends.

5 Pull the furry foam over the thorax and tie it down ensuring that the furry, not the foam, side is uppermost. Trim out the excess furry foam, wind a neat head ending with a whip finish. Trim out the thread and carefully varnish the whip.

Both Furry Foam and Crystal Hair are Lure-flash products.

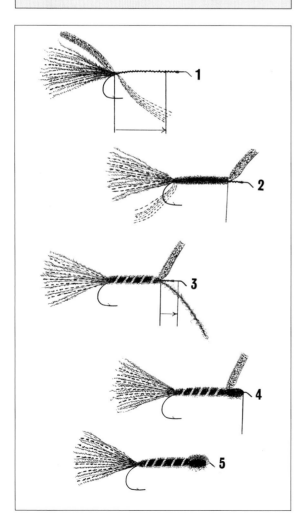

35 G.R.P. Nymph *(Freddie Rice)*

(General representative pattern)

MATERIALS

Hook	Partridge, code A, size 10, 12 or 14
Thread	Olive
Tail	Fine tips of body material
Body	Four to six swan or goose primary fibres dyed medium olive, black, claret, buff/yellow or, natural grey heron
Thorax	Dark olive seal fur, some hairs being picked out
Wing cases	Thick ends of body material laid over thorax

Tying Operations

1 Wind on a few turns of thread at the bend then tie in the body fibres with fine points extending beyond the bend for 3–5mm ($\frac{1}{8}$–$\frac{3}{16}$in), no more.

2 Pull the body fibres to the left and wind the thread in close turns over two-thirds of the length of the hook shank and leave it hanging there.

3 Wind on the long body fibres in close turns thickening slightly towards the point where the thread hangs. *Do not remove* excess fibre ends which should extend upwards.

4 Sparingly wax the thread and dub on the dark olive seal fur, not too thickly.

5 Pull the wing cases out of the way to the left and wind on the seal fur already on the thread building up a thorax hump. Leave the thread hanging behind the eye.

6 Pull the wing cases forward over the thorax to the eye and tie these down. Trim any surplus fibres left.

7 Build up a neat head, add a whip finish, trim the thread and varnish the whip. Then, with a dubbing needle or similar, pick out some of the longer hairs of the seal fur.

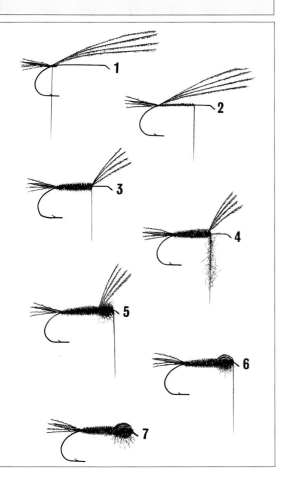

36 *Gold Head Caddis* (*Roman Moser*)

MATERIALS

Hook	Partridge, code CS2O, barbless, size 12
Thread	Brown
Weight	Fine lead wire over level shank
Body	Grey Irisé Dub which has irridescent Antron fibres
Head	Brass bead (or gold glass bead)

This pattern imitates the drifting and struggling pupa trying to rise to the surface. The gold head represents the gas bubble of the emerging pupa.

Tying Operations

1 Pass the bead over the shank and position it a little behind the eye and secure it there with Araldite or Superglue. Next, wind on lead wire in close turns over the level area of the hook shank.

2 Secure the thread behind the gold head then wind it back and forth binding down the lead and securing it in place, the thread to end up above the barb.

3 Dub the body material on to the thread.

4 Wind the dubbed thread over the lead underbody to behind the bead. Strip out any excess dubbing and whip finish behind the bead. Finally, trim out the thread.

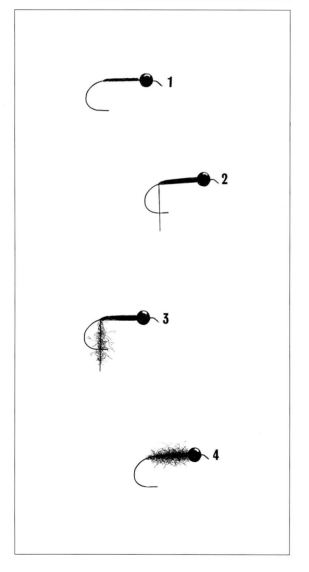

36 Gold Head Caddis

37 Gold Ribbed Hare's Ear

38 June and July Nymph

37 Gold Ribbed Hare's Ear *(Traditional)*

MATERIALS

Hook	Partridge code A, down eye, size 14 or 16
Thread	Primrose
Tails	Longish, light-coloured hairs from hare's ear
Body	Hare's fur dubbed on to the thread, ear fur nearest the bend, longer darker fur fibres from hare's body nearest the eye of the hook
Body rib	Oval gold tinsel or fine flat gold tinsel

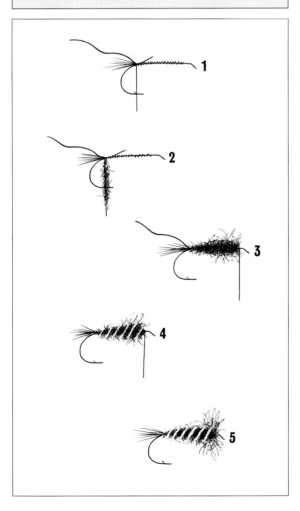

Tying Operations

1 Tie in the thread behind hook eye and then wind it in close turns to above the barb. At that point, tie in the tail fibres (natural points extending approximately 5mm ($\frac{3}{16}$in) beyond the bend) and the oval gold tinsel.

2 Preferably pick or, alternatively, cut the fur from the ear and wax the thread. Then dub the ear fur, not too thickly, onto the waxed thread.

3 Wind on the dubbed fur. A second dubbing of fur may well be necessary to complete the fly and this should include some of the longer, darker hairs. Tie off behind the eye.

4 Wind on the tinsel tightly in open turns to behind the eye and tie off. Remove surplus tinsel, add a whip finish, trim thread and varnish the head.

5 Using a dubbing needle, or similar instrument, pick out a few of the longer hairs at the eye end.

38 *June and July Nymph* *(G.E.M. Skues)*

MATERIALS

Hook	Partridge code L3A or L4A Captain Hamilton, size 14 or 16
Thread	Pale orange, with colourless wax applied
Whisks	Two strands darkish unfreckled cock guinea fowl neck, short
Abdomen	Three or four strands of pale heron coloured olive. Picric acid treatment originally used
Thorax	English squirrel blue fur or dark hare's ear
Hackle	Darkish blue, cock, short, one or two turns only

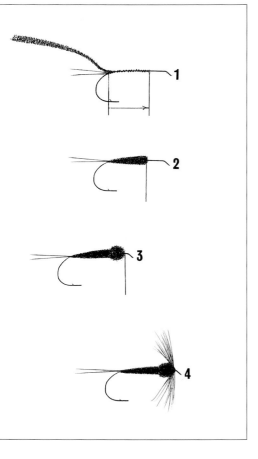

Tying Operations

1 Wind the thread from a little behind the eye to above the barb where the whisks are tied in to reach 5mm ($\frac{3}{16}$in) beyond the tying in point. That done, tie in the strands of heron for the abdomen and wind the thread two-thirds of the way up the shank.

2 Wind on the heron strands to where the thread hangs thickening the abdomen as you approach the eye end. Tie off and trim excess heron ends.

3 Dub the fur selected for the thorax to the thread and wind it on, not too bulkily.

4 Select the hackle and, after stripping the fluffy fibres from the base, tie it in on the eye side of the thorax and wind one or, at most, two turns. Tie off, trim hackle tip and butt end, wind a neat head, whip finish and trim out the thread.

This pattern was taken from *Nymph Fishing for Chalk Stream Trout* (1939), and on the original the hook Skues specified was a 'No. 1 down-eyed, round bend, or No. 15 or 16 down-eyed Pennell sneck'. Snecked hooks are seldom used in practical fishing now. The conversion to the Partridge code L3A or L4A is mine but the colour photograph shows, apart from the hook, the original materials precisely.

39 *Leadhead Grayling Bug* (Hans van Klinken)

MATERIALS

Hook	Partridge code H1A or E1A, size 10 or 12
Thread	Sparton Micro, brown
Tag	Fluorescent green Flexibody, four turns
Tail or legs	26mm (1in) mottled soft hen pheasant wing wound as a collar
Body	Rabbit fur well picked out
Head	Lead shot substitute glued with Superglue or Araldite

Tying Operations

1 Pinch a split shot in the centre of a 4cm (1¾in) length of 6lb breaking strain nylon monofilament.

2 With the split in the shot upright and facing over the eye tie down the nylon overhanging the eye, then whip finish and trim out the thread and waste nylon end. Retie the thread on the bendside of the shot, pull the nylon over the shot and bind it tightly down to the shank.

3 Wind the thread to a point above the barb, binding down the nylon leg as you go.

4 Tie in a short length of flexibody then wind the thread forward a little.

5 Wind on the flexibody four turns, tie off and trim out surplus.

6 Tie in the hen pheasant wing feather by its butt end.

7 Next, using hackle pliers or fingers, wind on the pheasant wing feather as a collar in front of the Flexibody tag so that the points overhang the hook bend but not so dense as to hide the tag. Tie off and trim out any excess fibres.

8 Form a dubbing loop (see page 7), insert twister followed by fur into the loop and twist the threads to form a narrow band of dubbing ready to wind on. Wind the single core thread to behind the split shot.

9 Wind on the dubbed fur forming a body of reasonable proportions to where the thread hangs. Tie off, trim out any excess dubbing loop form a neat whip finish behind the split shot and trim out the thread. Finally, pick out the dubbed body a little with a dubbing needle or use a Velcro pad to rough it up somewhat.

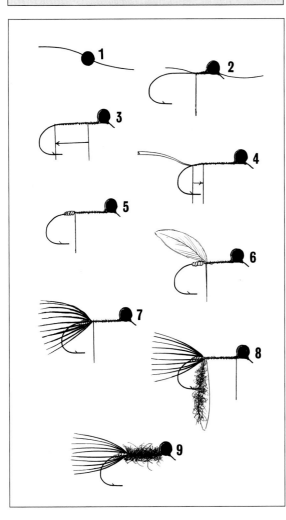

39 *Leadhead*
Grayling Bug

40 *Mayfly Nymph*

41 *Montana Nymph*

40 *Mayfly Nymph* (Richard Walker)

MATERIALS

Hook	Partridge code H1A long shank, down eye, size 8
Thread	Brown
Underbody	Unweighted type, light coloured floss. Weighted type, three to five layers of wine bottle lead
Tails	Five cock pheasant centre tail fibres
Overbody	One strand of very pale buff wool, angora is best
Overbody rib	One strand of medium warm brown nylon thread
Wing cases	Eight to ten pheasant fibres as tails

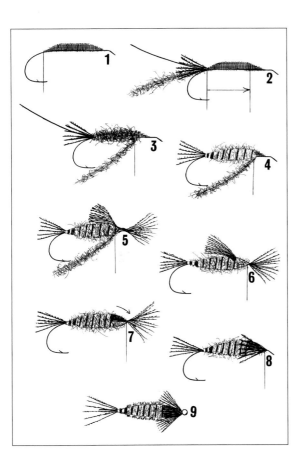

Tying Operations

1 For unweighted type, build up an underbody of floss. For a weighted type, cut wine bottle lead into strips 25mm (1in) by 2mm ($\frac{1}{16}$in). Lay a bed of closely wound thread over the shank. Add successive layers of shortening lead over the shank and bind down each in turn, the working thread ending above the hook barb. Coat the whole underbody with varnish and allow to dry.

2 Tie in the tail fibres with the points ending 7mm ($\frac{1}{4}$in) beyond the hook bend. Then tie in the strand of wool and the nylon ribbing thread. Wind the working thread to the position shown.

3 Wind the wool in close turns to where working thread hangs. Tie off but *do not* trim excess wool.

4 Use the brown nylon thread to form a band of five *close* turns, then a small space, then another band of four *close* turns, after which six *open* turns are laid on to where the working thread hangs. Tie off and trim nylon ribbing thread.

5 Cut about ten cock pheasant fibres, lay them *over* the shank (so that the points extend far enough beyond the eye to bend back later to provide the legs) and tie them in.

6 Wind the wool over the centre of the pheasant fibres for the thorax. Tie off and trim wool end.

7 Pull the butt ends of the pheasant fibres over the shank and tie them down behind the eye. Carefully trim butt ends, not the natural tips.

8 Divide the pheasant fibres beyond the eye into two equal bunches, bend them back along each side of the body and secure them there. Trim thread, whip finish and varnish.

9 Using a dubbing needle, pick out the wool fibres along each *side* of the body then clip them so that all are of equal length. Finally, run a streak of varnish along the upper and lower surfaces of the abdomen and the under side of the thorax. Do not spoil the side fibres.

Use a size 8 hook from early May to mid-June but much smaller sizes from early August.

41 *Montana Nymph* *(Traditional, US)*

MATERIALS

Hook	Partridge code H1A, long shank, down eye, size 6, 8 or 10
Thread	Black
Tail	Black hen hackle fibres or black marabou tufts
Rear body	Three black ostrich herls or one strand black chenille
Front body	Yellow or lime-green chenille
Hackle	Black cock wound over front body only
Wing cases	Ends of black ostrich/chenille

Tying Operations

1 Wind on the thread from behind the eye to start of the bend. Tie in tail fibres to extend a little beyond the bend and then the chenille or ostrich herls. Then wind the thread two-thirds of the way along the shank.

2 Wind on ostrich herl or chenille in close turns to where the thread hangs and secure. Do not trim the surplus. Select and tie in a black hackle and a length of yellow or lime-green chenille. Then wind the thread to just short of the eye.

3 Wind on the yellow or lime-green chenille in close turns to where the thread hangs. Tie off and trim surplus.

4 Wind on the hackle in open turns to where the thread hangs. Tie off and trim surplus hackle ends remaining.

5 Pull the ostrich herls, or chenille, down over the front body ensuring that the hackle fibres are separated when doing so. Tie down at the eye to form wing cases. Trim out ostrich or chenille surplus. Wind a neat head, add a whip finish, trim out the thread and varnish the head.

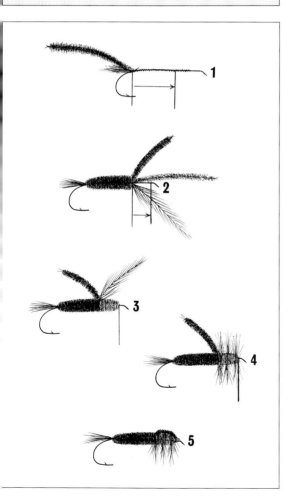

42 *Olive Shrimp* (Freddie Rice)

MATERIALS

Hook	Partridge code K4A Grub/Shrimp, size 12 or 14
Thread	Olive
Weight	Three strips of lead wire reducing in size
Shell back	Pre-stretched polythene or pale olive plastic raffia (Raffene)
Segmenter	Doubled thread
Body	Medium or light olive seal fur, rabbit or similar
Head	Thread

Tying Operations

1 If lead is to be added, lay the first strip on top of the shank and bind it down. Follow this with two more strips reducing in size then wind the thread well round the bend as shown.

2 Pull 15cm (6in) of thread from the shank and make a dubbing loop (see page 7) then secure the loop at the shank. Next tie in a hackle approximately 5cm (2in) long by its tip and a strip of polythene pre-stretched from a 6mm (¼in) width.

3 Dub the body fur on to the thread then wind it on in close turns to 3mm (⅛in) from the eye.

4 Wind on the hackle in five open turns to where the thread hangs, tie off and trim out hackle butt.

5 Trim out all the hackle fibres from the top of the body then pull the shell back polythene (or raffia) over the body and tie this down behind the eye. Trim out waste end at the eye.

6 Pick up the loop of thread hanging at the bend, twist it well to produce a single form of twisted thread and wind this over the body five or six turns, parting the hackle fibres as you do so to prevent them being flattened. Tie off at the eye, trim out the remains of the twisted loop, wind a neat head ending with a whip finish. Trim out the thread and varnish the whip.

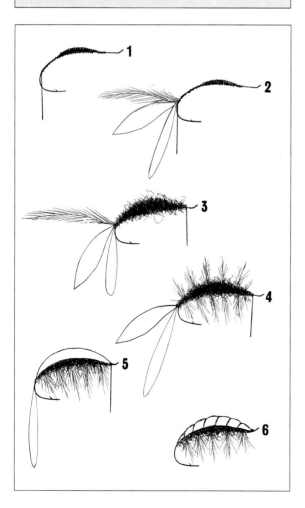

 PATTERNS

42 Olive Shrimp

43 Orange Sedge Pupa

44 Pheasant Tail Nymph

43 *Orange Sedge Pupa* *(Freddie Rice)*

MATERIALS

Hook	Partridge code K4A, size 8, 10 or 12
Thread	Orange
Body	Orange suede chenille
Thorax cover	Cock pheasant centre tail fibres
Horns	Formed by using the two outside fibres described for thorax cover
Thorax	Orange polypropylene, seal fur or similar material
Legs	About eight brown partridge back fibres

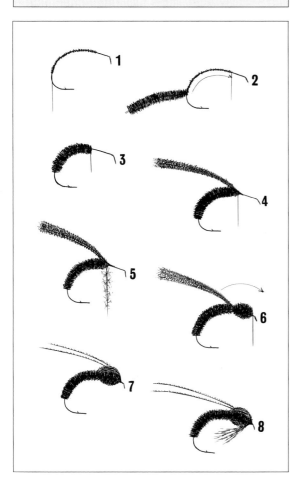

Tying Operations

1 Wind on the thread from behind the eye to well round the bend.

2 Trim the end of the chenille to a point and tie it in then wind the thread two-thirds of the way back to the eye.

3 Wind on the chenille in close turns to where the thread hangs. Tie off and trim the surplus chenille.

4 Cut out the pheasant tail fibres and tie these in *by the cut ends* so that they lie over the body.

5 If using *seal fur*, well wax the thread and dub fur on to it. Wind on the dubbed fur forming the thorax. Remove excess. If using *polypropylene*, cut about 20mm (¾in) and tie this in at the eye end of the body. Wrap it (as in dubbing) well around the thread and wind this on, forming the thorax. Remove any excess.

6 Pull the thorax cover fibres forward over the thorax and tie down. Then, select the fibre nearest to you and that furthest away and bend them back over the body forming horns and tie down.

7 The remainder are now trimmed out cleanly behind the eye as in illustration 7.

8 Turn the fly upside down in the vice. Gather the partridge back fibres and tie them in as a beard. Trim any unwanted ends over the eye. Wind a neat head ending with a whip finish. Trim the thread and varnish the head and whipping.

Using the Fly

When a rise to sedges is on, the fly should be moved in slow pulls *just below* the surface for which purpose the leader needs to be thoroughly degreased.

44 *Pheasant Tail Nymph* (*Arthur Cove*)

MATERIALS

Hook	Partridge code A normal, or code H1A long shank, down eye, size 8, 10, 12 or 14
Thread	Brown or black
Body	Six to 10 long cock pheasant centre tail fibres, depending on size of hook
Rib	Copper wire
Thorax	Natural blue/grey rabbit underfur, dubbed on
Wing cases	Ends of body fibres doubled over thorax

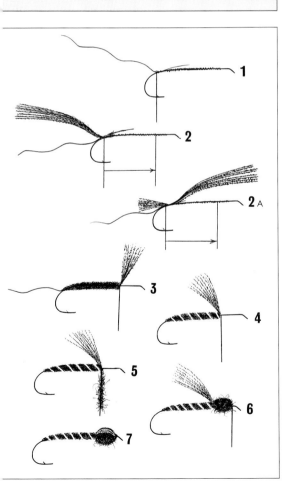

Tying Operations

1 Wind the thread from behind the eye to above the barb at which point the copper wire for the rib is tied in, the short end towards the eye.

2 Select the centre tail fibres, cut these to give maximum length and tie them in above the barb, the short ends towards the eye.

2A If you prefer a tail on the fly, tie in the centre tails as in 2A. For both types, next wind the thread three quarters of the way back along the shank.

3 Gather the centre tail fibres and wind these on clockwise and edge to edge, as a bunch or twisted into a rope. Tie off when the hanging thread is reached but *do not* trim fibre ends, just secure them so that they project upwards.

4 Wind on the ribbing wire in six anti-clockwise open turns to form seven segments to the body. Tie off and trim out excess wire.

5 Dub on *thinly* the rabbit underfur, ready for winding.

6 Wind on the dubbed underfur forming a pea-like thorax.

7 Pull the ends of the cock pheasant fibres over the thorax and tightly down behind the eye. Tie off, trim any fibre ends remaining, wind a neat head ending with a whip finish and trim out the thread. Then varnish the head.

Variations

For use in a sedge hatch, substitute lime-green, yellow, buff or orange dyed fur for the thorax.

To produce a general purpose nymph use olive dyed goose or swan fibres for the body and wing cases and use the copper rib and dark olive or brown underfur to replace the thorax grey. This is an excellent fly, widely used and acknowledged as the brilliant brain child of a first class nymph expert.

45 Pheasant Tail Nymph

47 Stick Fly

48 Suspender Nymph

 PATTERNS

49 The Shrimper

51 Adult Black Buzzer

52 BP Buzzer

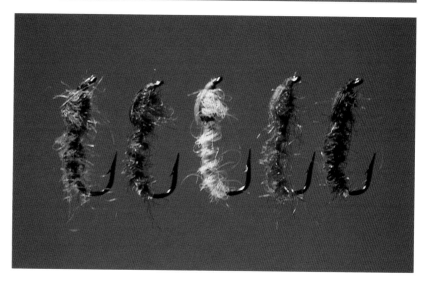

45 *Pheasant Tail Nymph* (Frank Sawyer)

(To represent various Olives:)

MATERIALS

Hook	Partridge code A, down eye, size 10, 12 or 14
Thread	None, body wire used instead
Body	Fine red-bronze copper wire, sometimes ribbed with silver wire
Tails, overbody & thorax	Four to six browny-red cock pheasant centre tail fibres, the longer the better

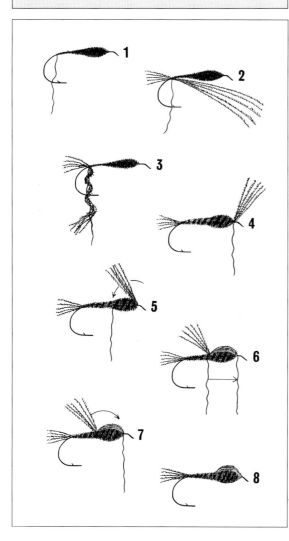

Tying Operations

1 Wind on the copper wire in tight, touching turns from start of the hook bend to just before the eye. Then form the hump for the thorax and work back to the start of the bend. Make sure that the wire cannot rotate on the hook shank.

2 Select the cock pheasant tail fibres and tie these in, using wire, so that the natural tips, not the cut ends, stand out a little beyond the tying-in point and are over the bend, and splayed out.

3 Twist the long pheasant tail fibres round the wire as reinforcement.

4 Wind the tail fibres and wire, twisted together, over the wire body back to the eye. Then separate the pheasant tail fibres from the wire but *do not* trim either the fibres or the wire.

5 Wind the copper wire back to the bend side of the thorax hump. The separated pheasant fibres projecting over the eye are then ready for 6.

6 Pull the pheasant tail fibres to the rear of the thorax hump and tie them down using the copper wire. Then wind the copper wire back over the thorax to the eye in open turns.

7 Pull the pheasant tail fibres forward over the thorax hump and tie them down behind the eye using the copper wire. Trim pheasant tail fibre ends and finish with three or four *tight* turns of wire at the eye in place of the usual whip finish. The excess wire is then pulled very tight, so that it sinks into previous turns, until it breaks off.

8 The finished fly appears thus: the copper wire colouring should show in places and the upper part of the thorax, which imitates the wing cases, should be much darker than the rest of the body.

Variation

For the similar Grey Goose, change the wire to a gold colour and the tails, body and thorax to the wing feather of the farmyard grey goose. A few feathers have a lightish grey-green-yellowish appearance, darker nearest the quill – use these. Tie the fly in the same way as Pheasant Tail.

46 *Silver Pheasant Tail* (Chris Ogborne)

MATERIALS

Hook	Heavy wire wet, size 10, 12, 14 or 16 (I suggest using a Partridge code G3A Sproat forged wet fly)
Thread	Brown, pre-waxed
Tail	Cock badger hackle fibres
Body	Eight cock pheasant centre tail fibres, very dark, greyish melanistic. If unobtainable use pheasant dyed nearly black
Rib	Silver wire, six turns
Thorax	Broad, flat silver or pearly tinsel
Beard hackle	Cock badger hackle fibres (close to body, tied in last)
Thorax cover	Ends of pheasant tail fibres used for the body
Head	Brown thread

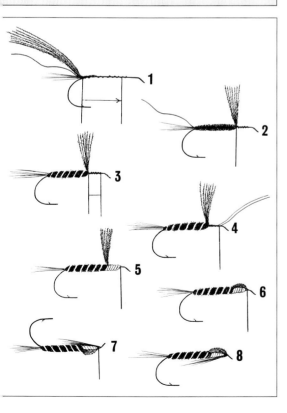

Tying Operations (colour plate on cover)

1 Wind on the thread from a little behind the eye to above the barb, at which point the tail fibres are tied in to extend a body length beyond the tying-in point. That done, tie in a short length of silver wire and the pheasant tail fibres by their fine points. Wind the thread back over two-thirds of the level shank.

2 Wind on the pheasant tail fibres to where the thread hangs. Tie off but leave the waste ends of the pheasant tail fibres projecting vertically. *Do not trim.*

3 Wind on the ribbing wire in six or seven open turns to where the thread hangs. Tie off and trim out excess wire. Then wind the thread to a little behind the eye.

4 Tie in a short length of flat silver tinsel behind the eye.

5 Wind the tinsel in close turns to the eye end of the body and back to where you started. Tie off and trim excess tinsel.

6 Pull the vertical pheasant tail fibres down over the tinsel thorax and, keeping them taut, tie them down behind the eye. That done, trim excess pheasant tail fibres projecting over the eye.

7 Whether the hook is turned over to tie in the beard hackle fibres is a matter of choice but keep the beard tied close to the body. Trim any hackle ends obscuring the eye.

8 Wind a neat head, whip finish and trim out the thread. Then varnish the head.

Variation and Using the Fly

In a later version, Chris Ogborne uses the pearly tinsel thorax but changes the tail and beard hackle to barred teal. Fished fast in the surface it is at its best and it is, he says, superb when the fish are chasing fry; it is also worth trying as the point fly on a team of buzzers fished slowly. A good all-rounder by the sound of it!

53 Collared Buzzer

55 Hatching Buzzer

57 Polyrib Buzzer

58 Raider

59 Surface Film Buzzer

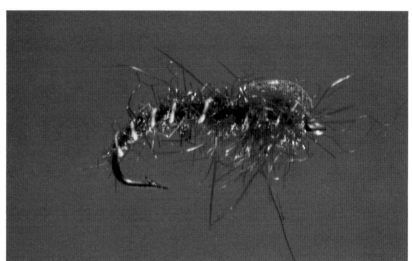

60 Waggoner's Grey Buzzer

47 *Stick Fly* (Sedge larva)

MATERIALS

Hook	Partridge code H1A, size 6, 8 or 10
Thread	Black
Body	Six to eight peacock herls
Thorax	Yellow, buff or amber wool or seal fur
Hackle	Ginger, honey or brown hen or soft quality cock
Head	Black

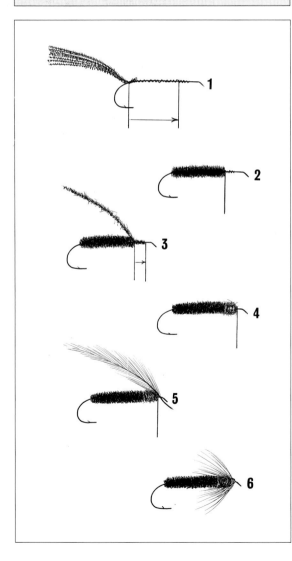

Tying Operations

1 Wind on the thread from behind the eye to the start of the bend where the peacock herls are tied in, the fine ends towards the eye. Next, wind the thread back to the position indicated.

2 Wind on the peacock herls, either in a bunch or twisted into a rope, over three-quarters of the shank. Tie off and trim out excess herl ends.

3 Cut approximately 10cm (4in) of wool, or dub on the chosen seal fur. If using wool, wind the thread to 3mm ($\frac{1}{8}$in) from the eye.

4 Wind on the wool or dubbed fur to a little short of the eye forming the thorax of the same bulk as the body. Tie off and trim out excess wool.

5 Tie in the hackle by the butt end to lie over the thorax and body, best side uppermost.

6 Wind on the hackle two turns only, tie off, trim out the hackle tip and butt end, wind a neat head ending with a whip finish and, finally, trim out the thread and varnish the head.

Variations

For Chew, this comprises the simple addition of a 3mm ($\frac{1}{8}$in) tail tag of fluorescent red or lime-green wool or floss.

For the Eyebrook caddis, the thread is brown, the body is of dubbed chestnut coloured mole fur, the thorax is a narrow band of greenish wool or floss. For the legs, add one turn of black or red game hen hackle.

48 *Suspender Nymph* (*Brian Clarke/John Goddard*)

MATERIALS

Hook	Patridge code A, size 14 or 16 (12 sometimes useful)
Thread	Brown
Tails	Three golden pheasant tippet fibres dyed olive
Wing pad	Ethofoam ball enclosed in nylon stocking mesh and coloured brown for which Pantone shade 499M is recommended
Body	Olive seal fur
Body rib	Fine silver wire
Hackle	Grizzle

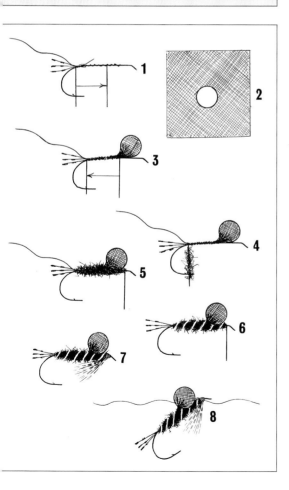

Tying Operations

1 Secure the thread a little behind the eye and wind it in close turns to above the barb where the tail fibres should be tied in followed by the silver wire. Then wind the thread to a point two-thirds along the shank.

2 Cut a 18mm ($\frac{11}{16}$in) square from a light-coloured nylon stocking (not her best pair!) and enclose the ethofoam ball within it.

3 Keeping the ball tightly enclosed, tie in the mesh ends on top of the hook so that it is held in place securely, then trim out any waste mesh ends. Next, wind the thread to the point of tail and wire at the bend.

4 Well wax the thread and dub on the seal fur ready for winding.

5 Wind on the seal fur clockwise, not too thinly, in close turns to a little beyond the ball. Lift the ball to do so.

6 Pick up the wire at the bend and wind this on in five to seven even turns. Tie off and trim out surplus wire.

7 The hook can be turned upside down in the vice and a bunch of grizzle hackle fibres, or a grizzle hackle tip, tied in to lie below the body. Tie off, trim out any hackle ends over the eye, wind a neat head finishing with a whip which varnish after trimming out the thread.

8 This shows the fly suspended below the surface by the ethofoam ball.

49 *The Shrimper* *(John Goddard)*

MATERIALS

Hook	Down eye Limerick, e.g. Partridge code J1A, size 10, 12 or 14
Thread	Orange
Underbody	Copper wire
Body	Brown/olive seal fur
Upper body cover	PVC or latex, widest at centre, but approximately 3–4mm ($\frac{3}{16}$in)
Palmer hackle	Honey

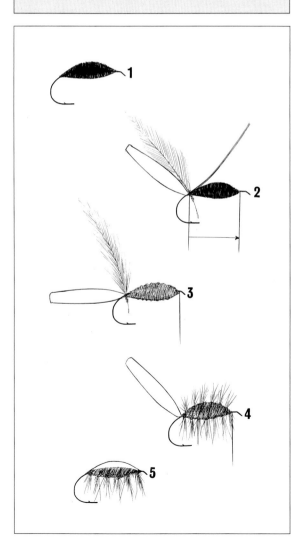

Tying Operations

1 Wind on the copper wire from eye to bend, thickening in the middle to a form hump, finishing with two tight turns. Trim surplus wire.

2 Wind on a few turns of thread at the bend then tie in shaped PVC, hackle and floss in that order. If tying the fly to show mating colour for June and July also tie in fluorescent floss after the hackle. Then wind the thread to 3mm ($\frac{1}{8}$in) from the eye.

3 Wind on the floss to cover the copper underbody and tie off 3mm ($\frac{1}{8}$in) from the eye. Remove surplus floss. (For *mating type only* wind on fluorescent floss sparsely, tie off at eye and trim.)

4 Wind on the hackle palmerwise (i.e. in open turns) over the body and tie off behind the eye. Remove surplus hackle tip and butt end.

5 Pull the PVC slip forward and down tightly over the body and tie off at the eye. Whip finish, trim thread and varnish the whip. Then trim hackle fibres from *sides of body only*.

Variation

In contrast, Richard Walker's shrimp pattern has fine lead strips laid as a hump along the top of the shank under an olive wool body. This turns the fly upside down to swim naturally. It has no upper body cover but the wool along the back is well varnished. A palmered ginger hackle is used, trimmed as for The Shrimper.

50 *Unweighted Caddis Pupa* (Roman Moser)

MATERIALS

Hook	Partridge code CS2O, barbless, size 10 or 12
Thread	Light yellow or primrose
Abdomen	Brown polyproxseal fibres or similar dubbing
Legs	Brown or medium red game hackle
Thorax	Creamy-yellow dubbing which incorporates sparkling fibres, such as Crystal Hair, to represent air bubble
Head	Thread

Tying Operations (colour plate on cover)

1 Wind the thread to the start of the bend where the brown abdomen fibres are dubbed on.

2 Wind on the dubbing to half-way along the level shank.

3 Tie in the hackle to lie over the abdomen.

4 Wind on the hackle three or four turns. Tie off and trim out hackle tip and butt end.

5 Pull 15cm (6in) of thread from the bobbin holder, lay on a finger at a 7.5cm (3in) mark then form the loop by returning the thread to the shank where it is wound to just behind the eye.

6 Select and spread out the thorax dubbing inside the loop, then clip on a dubbing twister and rotate this to trap the fibres within the two threads.

7 This shows the trapped fibres twisted in ready for winding on.

8 Wind on the trapped dubbing to a little short of the eye. Remove any excess fibres, tie off using the thread on the bobbin holder hanging at the eye, trim waste end of dubbing loop and wind a neat head ending with a whip finish.

9 Trim out the thread then trim out all the hackle fibres above and below the body leaving only those which project from each side of the body.

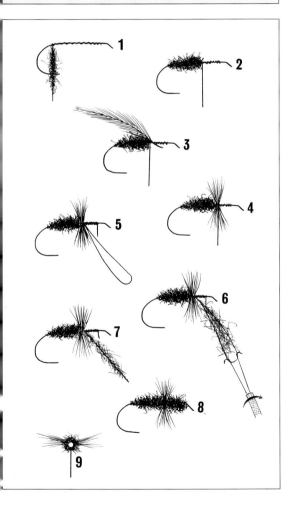

Buzzers

51 *Adult Black Buzzer* (Freddie Rice)

MATERIALS

Hook	Partridge code K2B, Yorkshire caddis, size 12
Thread	Black
Abdomen	Black dyed swan, goose, heron or crow wing fibres
Abdomen rib	A peacock herl stripped, leaving only the quill, or a black moose mane hair
Wing	A good bunch of dark blue dun hackle fibres
Thorax cover	Black dyed swan, goose or crow wing fibres
Thorax	Black rabbit or black mole
Hackle	Black eyed cock hackle fibres
Head	Black thread

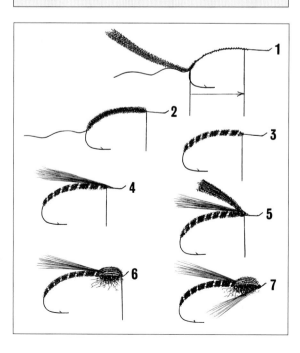

Tying Operations

1 Wind the thread from well behind the eye to half-way round the bend where the abdomen rib and six to eight abdomen fibres are tied in, in that order. Then wind the thread back to where you started.

2 Wind on the abdomen fibres to where the thread hangs. Tie off and trim out waste ends.

3 Wind on the abdomen rib in six or seven turns allowing flue to show through between each turn. Tie off and trim waste ribbing end.

4 Cut the wing fibres from a large dark blue dun hackle and tie these in to lie over the abdomen and reach 8mm to 9mm ($\frac{3}{8}$in) towards the bend from the point of tying in. Tie them in long and pull them back to shorten the wing to size. This helps to bunch them well together. Now trim waste ends at the eye.

5 Tie in a 4mm ($\frac{3}{16}$in) web of fibres (I used swan) for the thorax cover.

6 Dub the black rabbit or mole fur to the thread and wind on the thorax leaving room behind the eye to tie in the hackle. That done, pull the thorax cover fibres over the thorax and tie them down behind the eye, after which the waste ends can be trimmed out.

7 Tie in a reasonable bunch of black hackle fibres beneath the thorax for which purpose the hook can be turned upside down if this helps the operation. Trim out any hackle ends obscuring the eye. Finally, wind a neat head ending with a whip finish. Trim out the thread and carefully apply a touch of varnish to the whip.

A bunch of hackle fibres for the wing is longer-lasting than a pair of hackle tips. The bunch can be divided into two separate wings if you seek more realism.

52 BP Buzzer *(Gordon Fraser)*

MATERIALS

Hook	Partridge code H1A, long shank, down eye, size 10 or 12
Thread	Black on black, fawn on others
Abdomen	Blended fur
Rib	Clear polypropylene
Thorax	As abdomen
Wing cases	Hen pheasant tail fibres dyed to match abdomen

Tying Operations

1 Wind the thread one-third of the way round the bend where the polypropylene is tied in.

2 Blend desired fur and dub this to the thread.

3 Wind on the dubbed fur clockwise over three-quarters of the shank length.

4 Wind on the polypropylene rib in five open anti-clockwise turns. Tie off and trim any excess rib.

5 Tie in the pheasant tail fibres for the wing cases, then dub a little more fur to the thread.

6 Wind on the dubbed fur forming the thorax.

7 Pull the pheasant tail fibres over the thorax creating the wing cases and tie down. Trim out excess pheasant tail fibre ends, wind a neat head ending with a whip finish. Trim out thread and varnish the head.

I have tried this fly with fur blends of black seal fur and hare's ear mixed, claret seal fur and hare's ear, olive seal fur and hare's ear and claret and amber seal fur mix. All have taken fish for me, the black and claret types particularly. Also pearl tinsel has occasionally replaced the polypropylene successfully.

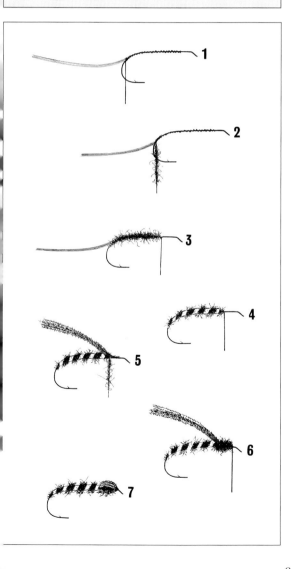

53 *Collared Buzzer* (*Chris Ogborne*)

MATERIALS

Hook	Fine wire Sproat or Partridge code A, size 12, 14 or 16
Thread	Orange or claret
Body	50/50 mix of amber and hot orange seal fur
Body rib	Fine gold wire
Collar	One to three turns of fluorescent red wool or floss
Head	One strand of peacock herl

Tying Operations

1 Wind the thread from a little behind the eye to just under half-way round the bend.

2 Tie in a short length of gold wire, then take a pinch of mixed fur and dub this thinly on to the thread.

3 Wind on the dubbed fur clockwise to a point half-way along the level shank. Remove any excess fur from the thread.

4 Wind on the gold wire anti-clockwise (four to five turns for a size 14 hook). Tie off and trim excess wire.

5 Tie in a short length of fluorescent wool or floss for the collar, then wind the thread half-way to the eye.

6 Wind a narrow collar of wool or floss to occupy approximately half the area between the dubbed body and the hook eye. Tie off and trim excess collar material.

7 Tie in the strand of peacock.

8 Wind on the peacock herl three to five turns forming the head. Tie off, trim excess herl, wind the thread through the herl to the eye where a whip finish completes the tying. Trim out the thread and varnish the whipping.

This fly is rightly described as a high visibility pattern incorporating, as it does, a collar of fluorescent red wool or floss to the rear of the peacock head.

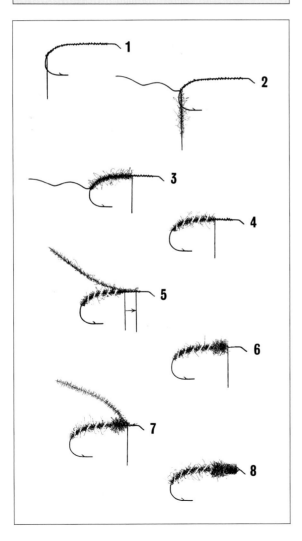

54 *Emerging Buzzer* (Freddie Rice)

MATERIALS

Hook	Partridge code GRS7MMB, Jardine, up eye Living Nymph, size 18 or 20
Thread	Fine, of a colour to match the abdomen
Abdomen	Four to six swan or goose wing fibres, black, orange, buff, olive or claret
Rib	Lureflash Nymph Wrap, clear
Wing	White rabbit fur, hackle fibres or Antron
Thorax	Rabbit or seal fur to match abdomen
Hackle	Small badger black, red game, orange, olive or blue dun cock
Head	Small, of thread with a three turn whip finish

Tying Operations (colour plate on cover)

1 Secure the thread well in from the eye and wind it to a point well round the bend where the abdomen fibres are tied in by their natural points, followed by a short length of ribbing. Then wind the thread to point 'A'.

2 Wind on the abdomen fibres in close turns to point 'A', tie off and trim out the excess.

3 Wind on the ribbing in five open turns to the eye end of the abdomen. Tie off and trim out excess.

4 Cut the wing fibres and tie these in at 'A' to lie low over the abdomen. Trim their length to 4 or 5mm ($\frac{3}{16}$in) and discard waste.

5 Dub the thorax fur to the thread and wind this on, not too bulkily, leaving room at the eye for the incorporation of the hackle.

6 Select the hackle, tear out the fluffy base fibres and tie it in at the eye end of the thorax and on your near side.

7 Wind on the hackle three turns, tie off and trim out hackle tip and butt end. Wind a neat, small head, add a whip finish and trim out the thread. Finally, trim away all the hackle fibres projecting beneath the hook as in illustration 7A and press those on top of the shank back toward the wing.

55 *Hatching Buzzer* (Freddie Rice)

MATERIALS

Hook	Partridge code K2B, Yorkshire Sedge, size 12, 14 or 16
Thread	To match body colour
Tail breathers	White rabbit fur, hackle fibres or DRF nylon
Abdomen	Swan, goose or heron wing fibres, black, orange, olive or claret
Abdomen rib	Pre-stretched polythene strip, Lureflash clear Nymph Wrap or pearly tinsel
Thorax cover	As abdomen
Thorax	Rabbit or seal fur, colours to match abdomen
Head breathers	As tail breathers

Tying Operations

1 Wind the thread from well behind the eye to half-way round the bend where the tail breathers are tied in followed by the rib and then the abdomen fibres. Then wind the thread to 4 or 5mm ($\frac{3}{16}$in) from the eye.

2 Wind on the abdomen fibres, ensuring that the furry side is outward, in close turns to where the thread hangs. Secure them there so that the remaining ends project vertically for use later as thorax cover.

3 Wind on the rib six to eight open turns, allowing the abdomen flue to push through, to where the thread hangs. Tie off and trim excess rib.

4 Tie in the head breathers to project over the eye, then take the thread back to the eye end of the abdomen.

5 Dub the thorax fur to the thread and wind a not too bulky thorax ending just behind the eye.

6 Pull the ends of the abdomen fibres over the thorax and tie them down at the eye. Then lift the head breathers and wind two turns to lift them. Trim any waste ends, wind a small head ending with a whip finish and trim out the thread. Now cut the head and tail breathers to length and pick out a few of the thorax fibres.

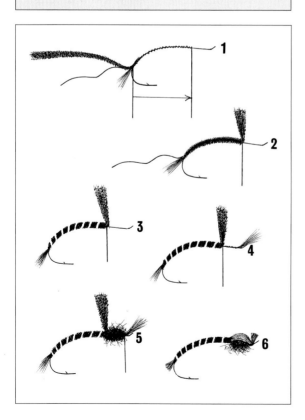

56 *Large Dark Olive Adult Buzzer*

(Bob Carnill)

MATERIALS

Hook	Partridge code A standard, size 10, or code K2B Yorkshire Sedge, size 12
Thread	Olive
Abdomen	Six to eight dark olive swan or goose herls
Rib	A natural peacock quill stripped of flue
Wings	Two cock hackle points dyed pale blue dun tied flat over the abdomen and slightly splayed
Thorax cover	A web of olive dyed swan, goose, or heron herls
Thorax	Mole fur dyed olive
Throat hackle	Sparse, olive hen

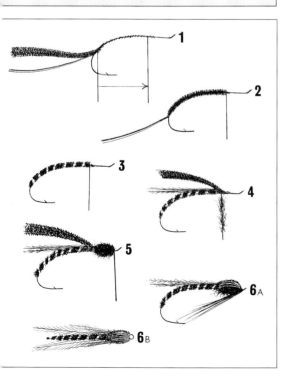

Tying Operations (colour plate on cover)

1 Wind the thread from well behind the eye to half-way round the bend where the stripped peacock herl and the abdomen fibres are tied in. Then wind the thread back to 6mm ($\frac{1}{4}$in) from the eye.

2 Wind on the abdomen herls in close turns to where the thread hangs, tie off and trim herl ends.

3 Wind on the stripped quill six or seven turns (to leave abdomen fibres projecting between turns) to where the thread hangs, tie off and trim quill end.

4 Tie in the two hackle points to lie horizontally over the shank with the tips slightly separated. Then tie in, close up to the wing joint, a 3mm ($\frac{1}{8}$in) web of herls for the thorax cover. Dub the mole fur on to the thread ready to wind the thorax.

5 Wind on the dubbed mole forming the thorax.

6A Pull the thorax cover fibres down over the thorax and secure, then trim any waste ends. Next, pull a reasonable bunch of fibres from the hackle and tie these in beneath (or above, if you turn the fly over for this operation) the body so that the hackle tips are reasonably spread and reach just beyond the point of the hook. Trim out any ends at the eye, wind a neat head ending with a whip finish, trim out the thread and varnish the whip.

6B Shows a view from above of the finished fly.

Variation

For the Large Ginger of Bob Carnill, the hooks are 10 or 12 code A or 14 or 16 code K2B. Thread is orange or golden olive (waxed), abdomen the same herl types but hot orange. The rib is the same stripped quill but dyed ginger and wings are as for the Large Dark Olive. The thorax cover is gingery-orange, thorax beigy-brown and the throat hackle pale ginger or honey hen. It produces an eye-pleasing fly.

57 *Polyrib Buzzer* (Bob Carnill)

MATERIALS

Hook	Partridge Yorkshire Sedge, code K2B, size 10, 12 or 14
Thread	To match chosen colour of thorax
Tail breathers	Three or four strands of electron white DRF nylon
Body	Swan, goose or heron, primary/secondary fibres, dyed to own choice of colour, e.g. olive, black, hot orange, claret, etc.
Body rib	Heavy polythene, stretched to 2mm ($\frac{1}{16}$in) width, about eight turns leaving gaps (about 2mm ($\frac{1}{16}$in))
Throax	Mole fur or synthetic fibres of a colour to match body, dubbed on
Throax cover	Feather fibres (swan, goose, heron, turkey) dyed to match body
Wing cases	Two broad, concave, white fibres (biots) from the *narrow* side of a swan primary feather either trimmed to shape before tying-in or with ends rounded after tying-in
Head breathers	White nylon baby wool secured with a figure-of-eight tying and trimmed close

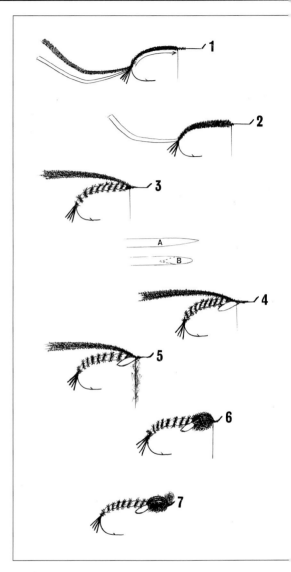

Tying Operations

1 Wind on the thread to well round the hook bend at which point the tail breathers, the body rib and body fibres are tied in. Then wind the thread back to position shown.

2 Wind on the body fibres to where the working thread hangs. Tie off and trim surplus fibre ends.

3 Wind on the body rib eight open turns. Tie off and trim surplus. Then tie in the feather fibres for the thorax cover.

4 Trim wing cases to shape and tie in, or tie in the untrimmed cases and trim afterwards.

5 Dub the mole fur or synthetic fibres on to the thread ready for winding on.

6 Wind on the dubbing forming the thorax, then pull the fibres (for the thorax cover) over the thorax and tie down behind the eye. Trim surplus fibre ends.

7 Make a small loose ball of nylon baby wool and tie it in between thorax and eye. Secure with figure-of-eight tying, wind a neat head, whip finish, trim the thread and varnish the head.

58 *Raider – Emerging buzzer* (Chris Ogborne)

MATERIALS

Hook	Fine wire Sproat or Partridge code A, size 12 or 14
Thread	Claret, pre-waxed
Body	50/50 mix of claret and fiery brown seal fur over two-thirds of shank area
Rib	Fine pearly tinsel
Legs	(Optional) Four knotted pheasant tail fibres, black, brown or grey
Thorax	Claret seal fur
Head	Claret seal fur

Tying Operations

1 Wind the thread from behind the eye to just round the bend. At that point tie in the length of ribbing.

2 Thoroughly mix the seal fur for the body then dub this on to the thread ready for winding.

3 Wind on the dubbed fur fairly thinly clockwise to a position three-quarters of the way to the eye.

4 Wind on the ribbing in six to nine open anti-clockwise turns. Tie off and trim out the excess ribbing.

5 Dub on a small amount of claret seal fur ready to wind the thorax.

6 Wind on the dubbed fur forming a not too heavy thorax.

7 Cut four cock pheasant centre tail fibres and tie knots 3–5mm ($\frac{1}{8}$–$\frac{3}{16}$in) from the fine tips. Then tie two fibres in on the near side of the fly, then the other two on the far side. Make sure the legs point slightly down and lie beneath the body to reach just beyond the outside bend of the hook. That done, trim out excess fibre ends at the eye end.

8 Dub a little claret seal fur on to the thread.

9 Wind on the dubbed fur to provide a slightly pronounced head. Tie off, wind a neat head ending with a whip finish. Trim out the thread and varnish the head. Finally, pick out a few of the longer fibres on the top of the thorax with a dubbing needle and trim them to leave short stumps.

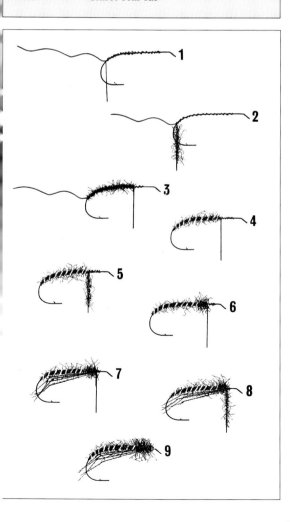

59 *Surface Film Buzzer* (Freddie Rice)

MATERIALS

Hook	Partridge code GRS12ST Emerger, Niflor finish, size 16
Thread	To match abdomen colour (claret type described below)
Abdomen	Claret seal fur
Rib	A stripped white hackle
Bubble	Red plastazote 3mm ($\frac{1}{8}$in) thick
Thorax	Claret seal fur
Head	Thread

Tying Operations

1 Wind the thread from well behind the eye to part way round the hook bend.

2 Strip the hackle of its fibres, then tie in the fine end of the quill securely. Trim out any waste short end.

3 Dub the claret seal fur on to the thread slimly then wind this on to 5mm ($\frac{3}{16}$in) from the eye, keeping the abdomen slim.

4 Wind on the stripped hackle quill in five open turns. Tie off and trim excess quill end.

5 Cut a short piece of plastazote 3mm ($\frac{1}{8}$in) wide, cut a short point in one end and tie that end in at the eye end of the abdomen, the long end to lie over the abdomen temporarily.

6 Dub more claret fur on to the thread, then wind this on to form a thickish thorax but leaving a little space behind the eye.

7 Pull the plastazote over the thorax and tie it down behind the eye. Trim out excess plastazote neatly, wind a neat head, whip finish and trim out the thread. Finally, pick out some of the dubbing on both *sides* of the thorax.

Using the Fly

With its plastazote bubble and the picked out thorax, this fly, when *lightly* treated with floatant, sits in the surface film and can be left to drift. Without floatant use it in the manner of the Bristol anglers with the 'top of the water technique' advocated by Chris Ogborne, the 1990 World Flyfishing Champion. Other successful colours are black, olive, or red/orange 50/50 mix.

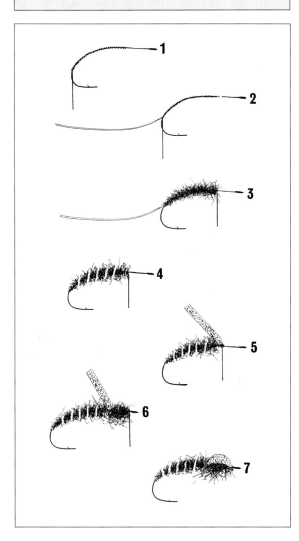

60 *Waggoner's Grey Buzzer* (Freddie Rice)

MATERIALS

Hook	Partridge code GRS12ST Emerger/Nymph Size 16, 18 or 20
Thread	Black or grey
Abdomen/ Thorax cover	A good web of light grey heron herls
Rib	A black dyed hackle stripped of its fibres to leave the bare quill
Thorax	Light grey rabbit fur
Head	A single strand of natural peacock

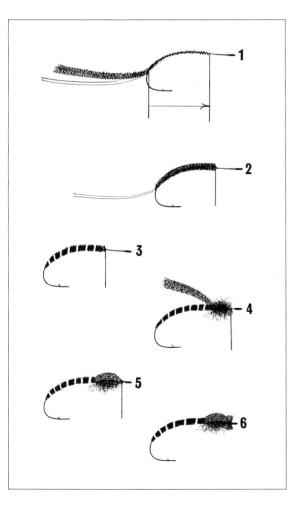

Tying Operations

1 Wind the thread from 5mm ($\frac{3}{16}$in) behind the eye to well round the bend where the stripped hackle quill, followed by a 5mm ($\frac{3}{16}$in) web of heron herl, are tied in. Then wind the thread back to 5mm ($\frac{3}{16}$in) from the eye.

2 Wind on the heron herls, ensuring that the furry side not the shiny side, is outermost, in close turns to where the thread hangs. Tie off and trim out the heron waste ends.

3 Wind on the stripped hackle quill in six to eight fairly close turns, allowing the heron herl to push up between, to where the thread hangs. Tie off and trim excess quill.

4 Close up to the end of the body, tie in a 4mm ($\frac{3}{16}$in) web of heron herl as for the abdomen. That done, dub on the rabbit fur thinly and wind the thorax hump, leaving a little room for the head.

5 Pull the herls down over the thorax and tie them down. Then trim the excess.

6 Select a single peacock strand from just outside the eye, tie this in on the eye side of the thorax and wind three close turns. Tie off, trim excess peacock strand, wind a few securing turns ending with a whip finish. Trim out the thread and varnish the head after pulling back the peacock flue.

Using the Fly

Many years ago I used to frequent some National Trust hammer ponds stocked with rainbows at Waggoners Wells, Grayshott on the Surrey/ Hampshire borders, where a terrific mayfly hatch occurred near enough to May 7 each year. When the mayfly hatch ceased the grey buzzers would appear and I produced this pattern for use there. Since then it has done well at Albury in Surrey, Pitsford Water in Northamptonshire and at Humshaugh in Northumberland, although only at Pitsford does there seem to be any record of grey buzzers being present.

ADDITIONAL DRESSINGS

Lures

Dog Nobbler Colour Combinations

(See dressing on p. 22)

Variant	Body (Chenille)	Tail (Marabou or Ostrich)	Body Hackle (Cock)	Type of Nobbler
1	White	White	White	Standard
2	Black	Black	Black	Standard
3	Chocolate	Black & Orange	None	Tiger
4	White	Brown	None	Tiger
5	Green	Green	None	Standard
6	Olive	Olive	None	Standard
7	Black	Black	Grizzle	Big Killer (Tiger)
8	Your Choice	Your Choice	Optional and Your choice	Dirty Dog

Bullet Minnow

A pattern from the USA.

MATERIALS

Hook	Extra long shank, size 4, 6 or 8
Thread	Red
Body	Flat silver tinsel
Underhead wing and tail	White bucktail
Overhead wing and tail	Natural brown bucktail

The wings are tied in initially to project over the eye, are then pulled back and tied down one-third along the shank to produce a form of rounded head.

Goat's Toe

A pattern of Irish descent.

MATERIALS

Hook	Standard or long shank, size 8, 10 or 12
Thread	Black
Tag	Gold or silver flat tinsel
Tail	Red or yellow wool or floss, short
Body	Red or yellow wool or floss
Rib	Bronze peacock herl fairly closely wound
Hackle	Green or blue peacock breast feather
Head	Black

Mickey Finn

MATERIALS

Hook	Long shank, bronze or silvered, size 6, 8 or 10
Thread	Black
Body	Flat silver tinsel
Rib	Silver, wire or oval tinsel
Wing	Bucktail or bleached and dyed squirrel, yellow over red over yellow
Head	Black

Orange and Gold Frog Nobbler

This pattern is by Bob Church.

MATERIALS

Hook	Long shank, size 8, 10 or 12
Body weight	Wine bottle lead in strips on top of the shank, well secured
Thread	Black
Tail	Orange marabou plume
Body cover	Gold mylar tube, small or medium
Head	Black

Filleted Finger

MATERIALS

Shank	Single Waddington
Thread	Black
Body	Flat silver tinsel
Rib	Oval silver tinsel
Wing and tail	Crystal Hair Orange CH8, Mother of Pearl CH14 or Peacock CH1 tied in at the eye end to reach 15mm ($\frac{9}{16}$in) beyond hook end of the shank. Tied down with thread eye side of shank clip
Head hackle	Hot orange cock, three turns
Head	Bronze peacock herl, three turns
Hook junction	Clear silicone sleeving
Hook	Any standard length shank with an offset, size 8 or 10 hook, clipped into rear of Waddington shank and silicone sleeving pressed over joint to keep hook in line.

Missionary

(Dick Shrive's updating of an old New Zealand fly)

MATERIALS

Hook	Long shank, size 6, 8 or 10
Thread	Black or white
Tail	Scarlet cock hackle fibres
Body	White chenille
Rib	Fine flat, or oval, silver tinsel
Throat hackle	As tail
Wing	Teal or silver mallard tied flat over the body providing a form of parachute action
Head	Black or white thread, well varnished

Nymphs

Box Canyon Stone

MATERIALS

Hook	Eagle Claw, 1197B, size 2–8 or Partridge Code K12ST, size 12, 14 or 16
Thread	Black
Tails	Two dark brown goose quill biots tied in a 'V'
Body	Black yarn, tightly twisted before winding on to provide good segmentation appearance
Thorax	Black yarn, tightly wound
Wing cases	Brown mottled turkey or cock pheasant centre tail fibres tied in over the thorax
Legs	Furnace hackle wound through the thorax four turns before wing cases pulled over

A fly somewhat similar in general appearance to the Montana.

Chompers

One of Richard Walker's patterns.

MATERIALS

Hook	Standard shank, size 10 or 12
Thread	Olive, black or brown
Body	Ostrich herl, olive, amber or white, four strands only
Wing case	Brown raffene, but olive or black as options
Head	Thread, well varnished

Green and Yellow Nymph

This pattern is by Tom Ivens

MATERIALS

Hook	Standard shank, size 10 or 12
Thread	Black
Body	Divide level shank into four, rear half is greeny/olive swan or goose herl, next quarter is yellow dyed swan or goose herl, and last quarter, nearest to the eye, is peacock

A fly for use at, or just below, the surface.

Claret Nymph

This follows John Henderson's pattern.

MATERIALS

Hook	Standard shank, size 12 or 14
Thread	Claret
Tails and body	Four cock pheasant centre tail fibres dyed claret, the tips form the tail, the rest wound as the body
Rib	Fine gold wire
Thorax	Very dark claret seal fur
Hackle	Dark dun hen, two turns only
Head	Thread

Amber Nymph

A pattern created by Dr. Howard Bell.

MATERIALS

Hook	Standard shank, size 10, 12, or 14
Thread	Black for large, yellow for small
Abdomen	Amber yellow seal fur over two-thirds level shank
Thorax	Brown or black for large, hot orange for small, seal fur or floss
Wing case	From tail to rear of thorax, of dark grey/brown fibre
Hackle	Hen, honey coloured, short fibred, as a beard

Little Mole

One of the author's patterns.

MATERIALS

Hook	Standard Shank, size 12, 14 or 16
Thread	Brown
Tail	Four olive hackle fibres
Abdomen	Olive, black or orange rabbit fur, slimly tapered
Rib	Tying thread, four open turns
Thorax	Natural mole fur
Hackle	Badger cock, short fibred, two turns only
Head	Brown and small

Drennan Midge

(By Chris Ogborne's Bristol Committee)

MATERIALS

Hook	Drennan Midge size 12 (Partridge code K4A as alternative)
Thread	Black or brown
Tail	Pearly 'Flashabou', tied well into the bend
Body	Seal's fur mix of hot orange, claret and ruby, tied half slim and half bulky to build up into a thorax
Wing	Hackle points from amber variegated cape, tied semi-emerger style
Hackle	Medium red game
Head	Thread

Note: Chris Ogborne observes that 'for fishing semi-dry, grease the hackle tips *only*. This is the essence of the semi-emerger patterns, in that they lie right *in* the surface film and present a perfect silhouette when viewed in the fish's window.'

Wobble Worm

Devised by Peter Lapsley.

MATERIALS

Hook	Partridge code K2B or K4A, Size 12 or 14
Head	No. 3 or No. 5 split shot crimped onto the shank immediately behind the eye and painted as body colour
Tail	A thin $\frac{1}{2}$in to $\frac{3}{4}$in tuft of green red or buff marabou to match body
Underbody	Silver tinsel for the red version, gold for the green and buff ones
Body	Very lightly dubbed red, green, or buff seal's fur, the red version ribbed with fine silver wire, the green and buff ones with fine gold wire

The Wobble Worm is already very well known. It is fished slow sink and draw by some but "jigged" in short, snappy retrieves by others. Both methods have brought limit bags.

Buzzers

Footballer

Geoffrey Bucknall's pattern.

MATERIALS

Hook	Standard shank, size 10, 12, 14, 16 or 18
Thread	White
Body	Alternate turns of black then white horsehair to half-way round the bend. Black and clear nylon monofilament over differing fluorescent flosses provide a number of colour options
Head	One strand bronze peacock herl

Cast the fly ahead of individual fish, let it break through the surface film and, after a three second interval, draw it in a slow pull.

Black Pearl Buzzer

Devised by Peter Lapsley.

MATERIALS

Hook	Partridge Emerger/Nymph code GRS12ST, size 18
Thread	Black
Abdomen	Four swan wing fibres dyed black, to part round the bend
Rib	Fine pearly tinsel, six open turns
Thorax	Black rabbit or seal fur
Head	Two turns white swan herl

Buzzer Nymph

Another of Dr. Howard Bell's patterns.

MATERIALS

Hook	Standard shank, size 10 or 12
Thread	Black
Abdomen and thorax	Black floss starting part way round the bend
Rib	Fine flat gold tinsel
Head breathers	A tuft of white floss projecting to the rear at 30 degrees to level shank
Legs	Six fibres bronze mallard tied in at the head and reaching just beyond the bend
Head	Thread, well varnished

Red Midge Larva

MATERIALS

Hook	Long shank, size 10 or 12
Thread	Brown
Tail	Six well bent swan or goose wing fibres dyed scarlet, the natural tips to overhang the hook bend by 10–15mm ($\frac{3}{8}$–$\frac{9}{16}$in) depending on hook size
Body	The long ends of the swan or goose tail fibres wound on to within 4mm ($\frac{3}{16}$in) of the eye
Rib	Silver tinsel, medium width, five to seven open turns
Thorax	Light brown or buff swan/goose herls

Bibliography

Ade, Robin, *The Trout and Salmon Handbook* (1989)

Chinery, M., *Insects of Britain and Northern Europe* (1972)

Clarke, Brian, *The Pursuit of Stillwater Trout* (1975)

Cove, Arthur, *My Way with Trout* (1987)

Fraser, Gordon, *Mastering the Nymph* (1987)

Goddard, J. and Clarke, B., *The Trout and the Fly* (1980)

Harris, J.R., *An Angler's Entomology* (1952)

Ivens, Tom, *Stillwater Fly-fishing* (1952)

Price, S.D., *Lures for Game, Coarse and Sea Fishing* (1972)

Price, S.D., *New Patterns – An International Guide* (1986)

Rice, Freddie, *Fly-Tying Illustrated – Nymphs and Lures* (1976)

Roberts, John, *The New Illustrated Dictionary of Trout Flies* (1986)

Robson, Kenneth, *Robson's Choice* (1985)

Sawyer, Frank, *Nymphs and the Trout* (1970)

Sawyer, Frank, *Keeper of the Stream* (1970)

Skues, G.E.M., *Nymph Fishing for Chalk Stream Trout* (1939)

Veniard, John, *Fly Dresser's Guide* (1977)

Courtney Williams, A., *A Dictionary of Trout Flies* (1973)

Scientific publication of the Freshwater Biological Association,

Macan, T.T., *A Key to the Nymphs of the British Ephemeroptera* (1979)

OTHER BOOKS OF INTEREST

Church, Bob, *Guide to Trout Flies* (1987)

Clegg, T., *Hair and Fur in Fly Dressing* (1969)

Clegg, T., *The Truth about Fluorescents* (1967)

Colyer and Hammond, *Flies of the British Isles* (1951)

Hills, J. W., *A History of Fly Fishing for Trout* (1973)

Lapsley, P., *The Bankside Book of Reservoir Trout Flies* (1978)

Walker, C.F., *Lake Flies and their Imitation* (1969)

Magazines

United Kingdom
Fly-Fishing and Fly-Tying
Practical Gamefishing
Salmon, Trout and Sea-Trout
Trout and Salmon
Trout Fisherman

USA
American Flytyer
Fly Fisherman
Flyfishing
Salmon, Trout and Steelhead
United Fly Tyers' Roundtable

Look and Learn by Video Film

Advanced Fly Tying, Peter Mackenzie Philps
Fishing the Caddis, Roman Moser (Flyfishing and Flytying)
Fly Fishing in Clear Water, Cockwill and Price
Fly Tying and Fishing for Trout, Bob Carnill
Still Waters, Benson & Hedges
Stillwater Trout from a Boat, Bob Church
The Educated Trout, John Goddard and Brian Clarke (The story behind the book called 'The Trout and the Fly')
The Game Fly, Andy Nicholson
Top of the Water Technique, Chris Ogborne (Flyfishing and Flytying)

Suppliers

UK
Partridge,
Mount Pleasant,
Redditch,
Worcestershire B97 4JE
Tel. 0527-41380/43555

Manufacturers and suppliers of all patterns of trout, salmon and sea hooks and superb cane rods.

Partridge USA Inc.,
P.O. Box 585,
Wakefield, MAO1880, USA.
Tel. (617) 245-0755

E. Veniard Ltd,
138 Northwood Road, Thornton Heath,
Surrey CR4 8YG
Tel. 081-653-3565

Everything for the fly-tyer – threads, tinsels, hair, plumage, books supplied wholesale.

Lureflash Products,
10 Adwick Road,
Mexbrough,
South Yorkshire S64 0BZ
Tel. 0709-580238
Fax. 0709-586194

Everything for the fly-tyer – threads, tinsels, hair and plumage. Catalogue issued.

Sparton Fishing Tackle,
Unit 2, Fields Farm Road,
Long Eaton,
Nottingham NG10 3FZ
Tel. 0602-463562
Fax. 0602-463571

All fly-tying materials including their famous 'Micro' thread, rods, reels, lines and other tackle. Catalogue issued, Britain's only float tube dealers and specialists.

Tom Saville Ltd,
Unit 7, Salisbury Square,
Middleton Street, off Ilkeston Road,
Nottingham NG7 2AB
Tel. 0602-784248
Fax. 0602-420004

Tools, materials, hair, plumage, rods, reels, lines, and other tackle, books and video films. Catalogue issued.

Sportsmail Ltd,
3 Allensbank Road,
Cardiff CF4 3PN
Tel. 0222-243166

Tools, materials, hair, plumage, new and used rods, reels, lines and other tackle, books and video films. Catalogue issued.

John Norris,
21 Victoria Road,
Penrith,

Tools, materials, hair, plumage, new and used rods, lines and other tackle, books and video films. Catalogue issued.

Cumbria CA11 8HP
Tel. 0768-64211
Fax. 0768-890476

House of Hardy Ltd,   Everything for the angler – rods, reels, lines,
Alnwick,   flies, bags and other tackle.
Northumberland NE66 2PG
Tel: 0665-602771
Fax. 0665-602389

Garry Evans,   Fly-tying tools and materials, rods, reels,
105 Whitchurch Road,   lines and all other tackle.
Cardiff CF4 3JQ
Tel. 0222-619828/692968

Farlow's,   Fly-tying tools and materials, flies, rods and
5 Pall Mall,   all other tackle.
London, SW1
Tel. 071-839-2423

Ron Taylor,   Rare plumage, hair and fur.
Rare Feathers Ltd,
Kaledna, Garras,
Mawgan-in-Meneage,
Nr. Helpston, Cornwall TR12 6LP
Tel. 0326-22391

Ellis Slater,   Rare plumage, hair and fur.
47 Bridgecross Road,
Chase Terrace,
Walsall,
West Midlands WS7 8BU
Tel: 054-36-71377

The Orvis Co. Inc.   Everything for the angler – rods, reels, lines,
The Mill,   flies, bags and all other tackle.
Nether Wallop, Stockbridge,
Hampshire SO20 8ES
Tel. 0264-781212

USA
The Orvis Co. Inc.,
Manchester,
Vermont 05254
USA

Danville Chenille Co. Inc.   A wide range of chenilles and fly-tying
P.O. Box 1000,   threads.
Danville, NH 03819, USA

Societies of Interest

Anglers Co-operative Association,
23 Castlegate,
Grantham,
Lincolnshire NG31 6SW

Fly Dressers Guild,
Mr. P.C. Kerley, Honorary Secretary,
'Kumbayah',
8, Tidworth Road,
Salisbury SP4 0NG
Tel. 0980-610721

The Salmon and Trout Association,
Fishmongers' Hall,
London EC4R 9EL

United Flytyers Inc.,
P.O. Box 220,
Maynard,
Mass. 01754,
USA

And now we are arrivéd at the last,
In wished harbour where we meane to rest;
And make an end of this our journey past;
Here then in quiet roade I think it best
We strike our sailes and stedfast Anchor cast
For now the Sunne low setteth in the West.
John Dennys, *Secrets of Angling* (1613)

Index